10 for **Finding Families for Children**

Jennifer Cousins

Published by
**British Association for Adoption & Fostering
(BAAF)**
Saffron House
6–10 Kirby Street
London EC1N 8TS
www.baaf.org.uk

Charity registration 275689

British Library Cataloguing in Publication Data
A catalogue record for this book is available from the British Library

ISBN 978 1 905664 28 3

Designed by Andrew Haig & Associates
Typeset by Fravashi Aga
Printed in Great Britain by Athenaeum Press Ltd
Trade distribution by Turnaround Publisher Services, Unit 3,
Olympia Trading Estate, Coburg Road, London N22 6TZ

BAAF is the leading UK-wide membership organisation for all those
concerned with adoption, fostering and child care issues.

The paper used for the text pages of this book is FSC certified.
FSC (The Forest Stewardship Council) is an international network
to promote responsible management of the world's forests.

Printed on totally chlorine-free paper.

FSC
Mixed Sources
Product group from well-managed
forests and other controlled sources

Cert no. SGS-COC-2482
www.fsc.org
© 1996 Forest Stewardship Council

Contents

Note about the author

Jennifer Cousins is the consultant to BAAF's Opening Doors Disability Project. She has been a child placement consultant and trainer with BAAF since 1997, based in the Midlands office.

Jennifer has extensive practice experience in family placement and children's disability, including a short breaks scheme and a multi-disciplinary child development centre. Her research degree examined the marginalisation of birth fathers in the adoption process. Since joining BAAF, her direct contact with practice has been maintained through chairing an adoption and fostering panel.

Jennifer is the author of the controversial article, 'Are we missing the match? Rethinking adopter assessment and child profiling' (*Adoption & Fostering* 27:4) and author of BAAF's Good Practice Guide on the placement of disabled children, *Every Child is Special* (2006), and co-author of BAAF's Good Practice Guide on the placement of babies, *Right from the Start* (2003). She has published a number of articles on social work themes in the national and professional press.

This series

Ten Top Tips for Placing Children in Families is part of BAAF's Ten Top Tips series. This series tackles fundamental topics in the areas of adoption and fostering with the aim of presenting them in a quick reference format. Each title presents ten good practice tips, each of which is then further elaborated upon.

Future titles will deal with leaving care and placing siblings.

*This book is dedicated to
Richard, Julie and all the children
for whom the system has failed to find
a family for life.*

Acknowledgements

Thanks are due to colleagues who enthusiastically sent me their "must do" tips for finding families. They are all incorporated here. I would also especially like to thank Hedi Argent, Jenifer Lord, and Mo O'Reilly for reading the draft so carefully and making such helpful comments.

This publication has been kindly supported by the Hedley Foundation.

Jennifer Cousins
December 2007

Introduction

This book is about finding permanent new families for children who cannot live with their birth parents or relatives.

In 2006, Bristol University published some shocking research findings. But nobody seemed to notice. The research team discovered that over a quarter of the 3–11-year-olds for whom adoption was in principle agreed were never placed with an adoptive family (Selwyn *et al*, 2006). If placement disruptions are added, it is evident that a significant number of children *never* achieve adoption, and are at risk of never having a permanent family at all. The consequent sense of isolation and disconnection is to most people unimaginable. This book is an attempt, through social workers and managers, to improve that situation and to help all "children who wait" to have permanent families, through whatever means, which endure through childhood and beyond.

The aim here is to identify some basic guidelines for creating an effective and imaginative permanence service. The intention is to provide staff who are new to the work with a framework – not to teach experienced staff how to do their job. However, some questions will be raised which only senior managers can tackle, and no apology is made for this. The ideas here will not fit all situations or be appropriate for all agencies: readers should pick and choose what might be helpful in their unique situation. One of the fascinating aspects of the UK social work scene is that, not only are we enriched by having a number of highly creative voluntary agencies, but also we have 230 local authorities which work slightly differently according to regional conditions and demands.

It is widely known that resources are always a problem, but unless staff at least aspire to improving services, despondency will set in. Throughout the text, therefore, an attempt has been made to be realistic about resources, but optimistic about agencies' capacity to meet some of the challenges. It often strikes me as curious that, with similar resources, teams respond differently: where one will appear depressed and demoralised, another will strain every muscle to be upbeat and innovative.

The emphasis in this book is on finding and sustaining permanent families – through adoption, permanent fostering and special guardianship. Although adoption has traditionally been the preferred route for young children, even that assumption should not go entirely unquestioned. An increasing recognition that permanent fostering is a valuable alternative for some children and the rise of special guardianship in England must prompt us to re-evaluate all forms of permanence as real choices for the wide variety of children who need families. Readers will notice that "long-term fostering" is not named here as a route to permanence and that "permanent fostering" is seen as a distinctly different form of care, though legally the same. This concept (permanent fostering) is not yet fully developed, and much work needs to be done, but to avoid confusion, some tentative definitions are given:

- **Long-term fostering** is not a truly permanent option. It fits somewhere between short-term fostering and permanence as an arrangement which is long-standing but not "for ever". Many long-term fostered children have entered care having lived well into childhood in their original family. They often still have strong ties with their birth family but are not able to live with them. A reasonable *modus vivendi* is achieved, and long-term foster carers know that their task ends when the child becomes adult, or before. In this book, long-term fostering is not described as a permanent option.
- **Permanent fostering** is legally no different from long-term fostering, but the intention is for a life-long relationship, where

foster grandchildren will be as integral a part of the family as the carers' own grandchildren. Although favoured by agencies for older rather than younger children, it is increasingly the pathway of choice for children for whom adoptive families cannot be found – even very young children. Agency support, which is available throughout the young person's childhood, is inevitably an attractive feature to potential carers who know that future placement complexities are almost certain. Permanent fostering also suits older children who do not want to sever the legal connection with their birth parents, but who definitely want to belong securely to a stable and loving family. In optimum circumstances this arrangement serves children very well indeed, and the outcomes are good.

● **Special guardianship** is seen as something of a half-way house between adoption and fostering, and has advantages from both. Although the concept may have emerged from considering the kinship network, a growing body of opinion is now developing around special guardianship as a particularly effective route for placement *outside* the child's network.

The special guardian has legal responsibility for the child without deleting the parents' legal tie, but will be able to take most of the major decisions about the child's upbringing. Special guardianship discharges the care order, so the child is no longer "looked after" by the local authority – a factor which many prospective carers, who favour permanence without the continual involvement of social workers, say they want. In addition, support and financial help may be provided at the local authority's discretion. Special guardianship ceases when the young person reaches 18.

With all these different forms of care, we know that one may of course develop into another: many "short-term" placements eventually become permanent, and many fostering arrangements later, and with due consideration, become adoption.

Although the focus in this book is on permanence, it is hoped that some of the tips may in fact be useful in the other family-finding arenas: both short- and long-term fostering, task-centred fostering and short breaks. The term "carer" may occasionally be used for both adopters and foster carers.

But finding families for children is not only about recruiting a wide pool of potential carers: it is about narrowing the search on behalf of a specific child – making a match. For this reason, the book focuses both on recruiting and preparing families and, in the second half, on preparing and profiling children. In Chapter 10, we come to the match itself. Because of the convergence of the two different perspectives, readers will find that occasionally the same tip is given in a slightly different form in more than one chapter.

Readers may be disconcerted to see that the book does not start with the child: after all, our most dearly held mantra is that we put "children first". In planning the book, it seemed sensible to start with the importance of telling the general public about the hundreds of children who need their care, and to think about ways to increase the overall pool of possible families. It is difficult to imagine how family-finding for a specific child could even begin without the public being aware of the generic adoption and fostering issues, so, rather than introduce the child's perspective at that point, it seemed more logical to continue exploring carer recruitment and assessment, and to come later to the needs of children.

No structure will be perfect and readers who wish can of course go straight to Chapter 6 and the child's perspective.

Finally, it goes without saying that, where possible, a child should be returned home if this is safe and feasible, and that friends and family should be canvassed to see if they could be supported to care for the child permanently. The ideas which follow assume that these basic steps have already been taken.

Jennifer Cousins
November 2007

TIP 1

Broadcast the message: recruit widely

Research carried out following the 1999 National Adoption Week (NAW) campaign identified that:

> *...the route to becoming an adoptive parent starts with an interaction between a person's motivation and any opportunity she or he has to develop this motivation.*
>
> *(Simmonds, 2001, p 2)*

Publicity therefore provides the opportunity for motivation to be stimulated into action. If the pathway from motivation to action is littered with obstacles, potential families will give up. If it is welcoming and facilitative, then families will stay the course. It is the duty of agencies not only to publicise the need for carers and to provide clear information, but also to be welcoming, professional and non-bureaucratic.

Publicise the need

The first step in the family-finding process is to ensure that the public knows that there is a national need for more adopters and foster carers in the UK. In fact, one of the most persuasive statistics is that at any one time there are as many as 4,000 children who are waiting for permanent new families. At this first stage of recruitment, the approach will be generic; "real" children who need families are not featured, and publicity material will show models only.

In designing a general awareness campaign, staff need to be reassured that, although results may not be evident immediately, this does not mean it is wasted effort. Posters and leaflets have a cumulative impact, and often it is never known what exactly has triggered someone's interest. During National Adoption Week 2005, an award-winning billboard was produced, which stated:

> *This poster has no permanent home. Like thousands of kids in care, this poster will be moved again tomorrow.*

Which it was – to another poster site. Just this simple act of awareness-raising will jolt some people into thinking further about adoption and fostering, even if the time is not right for them at the moment. This is often called the "dripping tap" approach. Analysis of the 1999 NAW campaign showed that only one-third of enquirers were actively interested in adopting a child at that time.

Managers investing in these broad-brush campaigns have to accept that the returns are never quite proven, and do not show up on any particular team's targets. There was a story recently of a manager who would not agree to fund publicity on the local buses because they travelled through the edge of a neighbouring authority and he didn't like the idea of some other team reaping his rewards! This is patently unhelpful.

One effective strategy is to capture people's attention through normal everyday activities – when they are visiting libraries, supermarkets and surgeries (see Macaskill, 1985, p 98); or through newspaper and magazine articles. University open days, attended by parents who obviously take an interest in their children and will soon have an empty nest, may also be fertile territory.

Use the media whenever you can
Although there is a good argument for such general messages to be conveyed on prime time TV and radio, and funded through public services broadcasting, this rarely happens. But making a relationship with your local newspaper and TV station and persuading them to run regular features about adoption and fostering pays dividends. Many of the adoptive families recruited some years ago by the London-based agency Parents for Children enquired as a result of publicity featuring children in *The Daily Mail*. Triseliotis *et al* (2000) found that over a third of the foster carers interviewed were attracted to the job through an item in their local newspaper.

In July 2007, the BBC ran a *Family Wanted* season, consisting of five 30-minute documentaries, co-ordinated with storylines in many of their dramas; specific appeal films of actual children waiting to be adopted; and a celebrity *Who do you think you are?* episode with Nicky Campbell tracing his adoptive family tree. He was also the "face" of the season. This was a strategy generated at national level, but it was taken up across the regions in local radio and television programmes, which maximised the coverage. At the time of writing it is much too early to estimate the outcome but it was an impressive campaign.

As illustrated by Beckett and Oni (2005), the last few years have seen a growing partnership between agencies and the media. UK-wide television series are invaluable in conveying the general messages to millions of people. Such programmes always need material and, despite all the hard work of getting permission and clearance to feature individual children, agencies must try to co-operate where possible: these are golden opportunities. Particularly successful were the partnerships like ITV's *Find a Family* (1989–1991) and BBC1's *A Family of My Own* (2000–2001). In 2000, following the broadcasts, more than 16,000 information packs were requested – many people enquiring generally about how to become an adopter or foster carer as well as about individual children. In that sense these programmes serve a valuable double purpose. An example of a specific outcome is Swansea Council, which, having participated in *A Family of My Own* in 2001, received 86 enquiries and eventually placed seven children previously described as "hard to place". Five of these children had been waiting for two to three years.

There are a number of other helpful observations to emerge from research into recruitment. Campaigns which emphasise the general characteristics of carers are said to prove successful, plus informing people in clear terms about the wider package of training, remuneration, support and career development which they can expect. Triseliotis *et al* (2000) found that over half of the current carers he interviewed said that they had been attracted to fostering through "word of mouth" – a finding which many readers will recognise. However, the bad news spreads as quickly as the good, and any tight-knit community is likely to get to know if the local agency is friendly, responsive and supportive – or not.

To reiterate, if you decide to court the media you must be prepared to give them real-life stories about children and families: human interest sells newspapers and television licences, and works in firing people's imagination. The media are less interested in general pieces about the subject, however worthy, if they are not illustrated by a real story.

Use National Adoption Week

National Adoption Week (NAW), BAAF's annual family-finding campaign launched in 1997, has been supported by national newspapers, such as *The Sun,* and by GMTV. National Adoption Week, which signals the general need for more adopters as well as featuring specific children, has a huge impact on the general public. In 2006, NAW staff commissioned 48,600 publicity posters to spread the word, and during the week there were 275 mentions in the UK-wide and local press, and 69 television and radio appearances. As a result, members of the public requested 5,000 information packs, and agencies reported receiving an increased number of enquiries during the week. All agencies should ideally contribute to this national effort to raise awareness, and take the opportunity of nationwide publicity to give a fresh boost to their own local campaigns and to remind people about children who need forms of permanence other than adoption.

BAAF can also help throughout the year: family placement consultants staff the advice lines each week-day and frequently signpost the public to the right agency and send out general information about adoption and fostering. Readers might like to look at some of this material, which can be accessed through www.baaf.org.uk.

Create a really good website

Agencies will benefit in their recruitment attempts if they have welcoming, informative and accessible websites. The advice about websites is to include a wealth of information which people want to know (this, after all, is why they are accessing the site in the first place), such as 'how do you apply to become a foster carer?' or 'can you adopt if you're not married?' But you also have the opportunity to tell people what you want them to know – so you might include information about the numbers and "type" of children in the area who need families: but don't overdo this aspect.

The website text is often reaching directly into people's homes, so it must be relatively informal and personal: this is not the place for impenetrable gobbledygook. And though it is time-consuming, the website must be kept up to date and refreshed periodically with new images, whilst keeping the familiar colour scheme and "brand". Too many photographs will take up inordinate amounts of memory and could take ages for some older computers to download, which can deter people from going further. Similarly, Flash graphics can slow everything down and put people off. Roughly half of computer-users put the key word into the search bar rather than navigating around the website, so each route must work efficiently. Experts also report that there is a "three-click rule" with websites – that is, if searchers fail to get what they want within three clicks of the mouse, they will end their search, and you may have lost them altogether. If users are looking for information via one of the major search engines, it is important for the agency's website to contain all the popular and key search words about adoption and fostering as this is then more likely to provide the route directly into the agency's site.

Websites are an invaluable adjunct to an agency's recruitment strategy but they clearly require resources and skilled programming. They must always of course contain the agency's contact details, prominently displayed.

Assemble a good publicity team

The agencies which have been most successful in recruiting adopters have employed staff with specific skills in marketing and advertising.

(Commission for Social Care Inspection, 2006, p 25)

Marketing staff not only have skills in presentation, but also know how to target specific groups and convey the "message" in irresistible ways. It is odd to think that social workers have long believed that they could be as effective as publicity specialists in designing and delivering recruitment campaigns, when they would never have accepted that other professionals could just "do" social work! So, assembling the right team of experts – even sharing them across agencies where smallness of scale is an issue – is an important foundation for future success in recruitment.

Marketing and publicity people talk about the ideal "marketing mix" which consists of paying close attention to what is known as "the five Ps": product, price, place, people and, in the not-for-profit sector, process. It is useful to see how a campaign might be broken down in this way so that due attention can be paid to each aspect. Marketing experts also refer to "above the line" activity, which is marketing which costs money, such as advertising; and "below the line" activity generated through good public relations which, for example, leads to getting free features in newspapers, or sponsorship of a campaign. Integrated processes are referred to as "through the line". An agency needs to think about all these aspects in order to maximise its impact. It is obvious that developing good relationships in the community is likely to be a highly necessary strategy where budgets are tight.

Dispel common myths

Fundamental to all campaigns which introduce the public to the idea of adoption and fostering is the need to provide clear information and to dispel the commonly held myths about the barriers. People must be told that you *can* apply to adopt if:

- you are single (male or female);
- you are in an unmarried partnership (heterosexual, lesbian or gay);
- you are married or in a civil partnership;
- you have been divorced and already have children;
- you are not British (but your permanent home must be in the UK);
- you are over 21 (there is no upper age limit legally, though common sense will apply);
- you are disabled;
- you have a health condition (but you, or your partner, need to have a reasonable chance of seeing a child through to adulthood);
- you have a criminal record – it will be judged individually except where it has involved harm to children, or other specified offences (Schedule 1 offenders are barred outright from adopting);
- you do not own your home;
- you are not wealthy (financial support may be available);
- you have other children living at home (though an age gap is preferable);
- you already foster the child.

Judgements on all these issues will be based on whether someone can do the task, not (it is hoped) on prejudice about people's lifestyle.

The right to apply does not mean the right to adopt or foster: a wide range of issues will be considered in depth, with the interests of children at the heart of the process. The important thing at this early stage is not to let any interested people rule themselves out based on misinformation. A very good book which explains the issues in more depth is Jenifer Lord's *Adopting a Child: A guide for people interested in adoption* (BAAF, 2006). Fostering regulations are such that there are fewer actual restrictions, but just as much common sense – see Henrietta Bond's *Fostering a Child: A guide for people interested in fostering* (BAAF, 2004).

Tell people that older children need families

It is also useful to promote the message that, although adoption is commonly associated with babies, many children in the UK who need new families are older. Only 15 per cent of children on the Adoption Register for England and Wales are under one year old – and a further 16 per cent are between one and two years (Adoption Register Annual Report, 2006). This means that there are over a thousand children on the Register who are toddlers or of school age. The Register does not represent the full story, but the general message is worth reiterating – that because the range and needs of the children are extensive, all sorts of people from all sorts of backgrounds are required, and should be made welcome to apply.

Involve men!

Research shows that women make up 93 per cent of enquirers to a general media campaign. There may be many reasons for this, but we should perhaps consider how to make campaigns more man-friendly. Even a simple but explicit message that men are very important for children would be a start – or focusing campaigns on places where men are likely to take notice.

Get the "adoption support" message across

It is widely known that, although post-placement and adoption support come at the end of the process, support must be signalled right at the beginning. No one will come forward to care for children with complex needs (especially to *adopt*) if they fear they will be abandoned to deal with difficulties alone. In fact, the National Adoption Week research referred to above showed that the two issues about which the public wanted more information were the approval process and what services would be available – particularly whether they would be able to get financial assistance.

Unfortunately the public is not yet convinced about the adoption support message – partly because it depends upon individual assessments of need, and partly because agencies themselves do not know to what extent resources will be available further down the line. Even where extremely damaged children are featured, the *Be My Parent* profiles usually contain the words "possible adoption financial support". Although this is all that can legally be said at this point, it does not inspire confidence.

Spell it out!

The Adoption Support Services Regulations 2005 in England and Wales strengthen previous legislation. It now means that local authorities should provide the following support to families where an assessment of need indicates that this would be helpful:

- advice;
- counselling;
- discussion groups;
- therapy services for children;
- training for adopters to meet children's special needs;
- respite care/short breaks;
- financial support;
- mediation services for contact;
- assistance in the event of a disruption.
- In addition, the family's financial circumstances must not be taken into account when travel expenses for introductions are paid, or when initial equipment and furniture is bought for the placement.

It is acknowledged that the right to an assessment is a far cry from entitlement to services, but social workers must at least help prospective families to understand that in good faith, support will be given wherever possible. Each local authority in England and Wales has an Adoption Support Services Adviser (ASSA) to whom anyone can go for advice. Adoption support services are being considered as part of adoption legislation in Scotland.

Although there are specific issues surrounding adoption support, the matter of providing support to foster carers, and telling the public about this, is also vital in attracting carers.

Explain the different kinds of care needed and take account of motivation

Somewhere along the line, you will need to explain the different forms of care which are required to meet the needs of the wide variety of children, and fine-tune your marketing according to people's varied motivations. In general campaigns, the explanations about the different types of care should be simplified and brief, but as the enquiries come in, further clarification will be needed.

Adoption is probably understood by many as life-long, but "permanence" is less obvious and special guardianship new to most. Prospective carers who enquire often know whether they want a child as part of their family and say it would be 'too upsetting to keep saying goodbye' to a series of children in short-term placements; others are clear that they are offering a valuable social service which would be more like a job. Some imagine a relationship which lasts for several years, but is finite; some want a permanent relationship but not adoption. Careful discussion will help an enquirer to clarify their motivation and select the pathway which suits them best. Understanding the variety of legitimate and different motivations among the general public is vital in informing publicity and marketing strategies. Should special guardianship be developed as a resource outside the kinship network for a wide range of children, campaigns to recruit carers to this role will need to be highly visible and to explain clearly the implications.

Offer a graded "entry" to caring

Any new task can be daunting and it can take time to build up confidence. Some people who are interested in permanent fostering or adoption may not feel able to take the full plunge straight away, but would feel comfortable about a short-term or part-time commitment. They could become a temporary/"task-focused" carer; or a "befriender", sitter or short-breaks carer where the young person would benefit from new relationships or where the birth family or foster carer need support or a break. These carers who are new to the system would develop their confidence, learn extra skills, start to understand how things work and, where permanence is sought, may even wish to become the child's new family.

A flexible approach to recruitment such as this would require a revision of organisational structures and inter-team co-operation. Prospective carers would be welcomed to enter the system at whichever point they feel confident and, with further assessment and support, would progress into different areas of caring as everyone sees fit. The logical extension of this is for agencies seeking *permanent* carers to put extra effort into recruiting *temporary* families. We know that many unmatched temporary foster carers already keep children permanently where other family-finding efforts for those children falter. Developing a wider pool of temporary carers, where better matching (particularly ethnic matching) is possible, might in the long run serve the interests of many children who later require permanence outside their birth family.

Respond to expressions of interest

In these stretched times, this advice is a counsel of perfection, but nevertheless extremely important: campaigns should only be run when there are sufficient staff to cope with the response. Research shows that enquirer satisfaction is based on:

- ease of contacting the agency;
- the warmth and helpfulness of the response;
- a sense of being encouraged;
- the authority and professionalism of the staff;
- the accuracy and consistency of the information given.

The downside is obvious: satisfaction plummets if the enquirer is made to feel their request is unreasonable, or if they receive conflicting information. The likelihood of prospective carers giving up in these circumstances is high. But people rarely seem to complain if the answer to their question is 'well, it depends upon...' as long as the subtleties are explained (Simmonds, 2001).

It is widely known that there will be a significant drop-out following the initial contact with the agency and that as many as nine out of ten prospective carers may never get beyond the initial stage. This tallies with Simmonds' finding that one year after the NAW campaign, only 11 per cent of people in the sample remained in the process. For some people, withdrawing at an early point is entirely appropriate, but for others, lack of follow-up by the agency is responsible for losing good people. There is nothing more disheartening for potential carers, and damaging to public relations, than to meet with a resounding silence following an expression of interest. We know that this happens.

All prospective carers must be greeted promptly and courteously and should never be left to wonder 'now what?' even where delay in processing an enquiry is inevitable. Simmonds (2001, p 15) writes:

> *There is evidence from this evaluation that more needs to be done to provide people with the right information relevant to their circumstances. In too many examples, people had to work very hard to get any information at all or to get a positive and encouraging response from someone who was interested in them.*

Consider the following recommendations from Simmonds (2001, pp 17–18).

- Establish a system and procedure for receiving enquiries.
- Provide good initial information so that people can decide whether to continue.
- The system should take into account all sections of the community, including the provision of information in different languages.
- Telephone access should be straightforward and should not have to go through a central switchboard.
- Calls should go directly to an adoption-knowledgeable staff member.
- Information requested by post should be sent within five working days; it should be comprehensive.
- The system should be monitored, including feedback from enquirers.

Filter the response

Proper though it is to "welcome all comers", marketing and publicity colleagues tell us that a response to a general campaign will have to be carefully managed. We know that not everyone can do this complex task of looking after someone else's child, and staff who pick up the general enquiry phone must be trained in sensitively counselling out entirely unsuitable people, or people whose offer is clearly too limited. This is difficult, even for the most experienced staff.

Be aware that under the new regulations, timescales operate for adoption enquiries (see Chapter 4).

Checklist for Tip 1

- Make sure the public in your area know that you need them!
- Use the national and local media whenever you can.
- Create a really good website.
- Assemble a strong recruitment team and include expertise from other professionals.
- Persuade your local traders and services to display attractive posters showing the need for new families.
- Dispel common myths at the earliest opportunity.
- Tell people that older children need families.
- Get the "adoption support" message across in the early publicity – and spell it out. The same is true for support to foster carers.
- Positively welcome a diverse group of people; mention specifics, such as 'you don't have to be married'.
- Explain the different kinds of care needed and take account of motivation.
- Discuss in your team whether you could offer a graded "entry" to caring.
- Make friends with your local newspaper and TV station.
- Make the case for regular public service broadcasts on national TV and radio.
- Use National Adoption Week to raise awareness. Offer to help BAAF: contribute case examples and good-news items.
- Find out more about BAAF's public information leaflets on adoption and fostering.
- Respond to enquiries from the public within a reasonable timescale.
- Keep people informed.
- Train and support front-line staff who need to tell some enquirers that their offer is unsuited to the agency's need.
- Keep in mind the necessary timescales so that enquiries are dealt with promptly.

TIP 2

Target your efforts

After raising public awareness generally, the next step is to refine campaigns so that the right families are specifically encouraged to come forward – the families which your agency needs.

Recruit only the families you need

The central tenet of family-finding is that adoption and fostering are not primarily services for adults, but services for children. According to Standard F6 of the National Adoption Standards for England, agencies have a right to prioritise their work:

> *Agencies will plan, implement and evaluate effective strategies to recruit sufficient adopters to meet the needs of children waiting for adoption locally and nationally, especially those from diverse ethnic and cultural backgrounds and disabled children.*
>
> *(Department of Health, 2001)*

As long as agencies signal very clearly in publicity what their criteria are, it is thought that they may legally turn away applicants who do not offer a resource they can use. For example, a voluntary agency may have eligibility criteria based on religious beliefs; or agencies may only need to recruit families for older children but are approached by baby-adopters. However, as this is currently a moot point, some people suggest that legal advice should be sought. Once an application form has been issued, the whole process must go forward unless the applicants voluntarily withdraw.

Show relevant images

The old belief that adoption is about white-UK babies still persists among the general public, while social workers in some areas will be struggling to place black and minority ethnic boys, sibling groups, disabled children and so on. Agencies will want to make an audit of the children who are waiting for families so that the images in publicity reflect this need and the public are properly informed. Child models will be used on posters and leaflets at this stage.

Use your local consortium

It is inevitable that the demographic profile varies between local authorities. Historically, urban conurbations were more likely to have higher numbers of looked after children, and rural areas more families offering themselves as carers. One agency could be turning away prospective families which another agency could use. In a national system which is more or less unco-ordinated, the dilemma has been mitigated to some extent by the development of local consortia: groups of agencies committed to working collaboratively in the interests of children. These should be supported.

With the interagency fee arrangement, the costs of recruiting and approving the carer-families are more fairly shared between agencies, though the higher fee required by voluntary agencies has been known on occasion to deter a local authority from selecting a voluntary agency's family for their child. Often in consortia, arrangements are made between local authorities for a "nil fee" where the balance of providing families/seeking families is equal.

Focus your efforts

Some very effective mini-campaigns were run some years ago along the following lines, described by Argent (personal communication). These ideas might be worth replicating.

● Gather together material about a very specific group of children who are similar in some way: for example, three girls who have Down's syndrome; or six boys aged 6–8; or four sibling pairs, and so on. (The consortium may be able to do this more easily.)
● Saturate a small locality with leaflets and material about one group of children. Your message is that they are people whom you need "on board". You will want to give as much information as possible to illustrate that, although there are some similarities between the children, they are as diverse as any group.
● Follow this up with an Activity Day (see Chapter 9) to see whether any real links emerge.

The main message is: focus, focus, focus.

Recruiting families for black and minority ethnic (BME) children

The term "black" is widely used as a generic term in reference to people whose roots originate in Africa or the Caribbean. The term "black and minority ethnic" (BME) is used as a general term to encompass both black and Asian people and those from, for example, China, Malaysia, Vietnam and various countries in the Middle East, as well as those of mixed-heritage (Rule, 2006, p 2).

The widely accepted view is that BME children should, where possible, be placed in a BME family, or a family which reflects their ethnic and cultural background. Children's identity, and support in facing racism, is believed to be optimised where at least one parent shares their background as closely as possible.

Many agencies, particularly in the major conurbations, struggle to find families for BME children – children who are over-represented in the care system. The Adoption Register has been particularly successful in initiating placements for BME children: they accounted for 41 per cent of the 159 placements facilitated in 2006. However, many of the children referred from BME backgrounds are very young and often have no additional needs other than for a family: they are disproportionately represented on the Register. The number of families on the Register does not match the number of children, and during 2006 the mis-match between BME children and applicants was 471 children to 212 prospective adoptive families.

Historically, targeted campaigns that engaged black communities worked best. The Soul Kids campaign of 1975 was the first of these, but more recently NCH London Black Families, among others, has made great inroads into recruiting black families. They have done this partly through dispelling some of the myths which deter people, and partly through making sure that the project staff and culture reflect the communities they are aiming to engage. Their applicants say it is 'like a breath of fresh air' to find that they are properly understood from the start (Rule, 2006, p 9).

Blackburn with Darwin adoption service worked with the Muslim Welfare Institute to raise the profile of adoption in the Muslim community by the following measures:

- running a seminar to increase understanding of Islamic perspectives on adoption and UK adoption law;
- holding an Eid Mubarak celebration for all adoptive families;
- appointing a member of the Muslim Welfare Institute to sit on the adoption panel and advise on cultural and religious issues;
- employing 50 per cent of the adoption service staff of Asian heritage, which facilitates effective communication;
- running information evenings and preparation training in Urdu;
- setting up an Asian adopters' support group and other social events.

(Commission for Social Care Inspection, 2006, p 27)

Employing black staff does not mean that only black staff should work with black families. However, an atmosphere of trust and understanding is more easily generated if black staff are in evidence to welcome new families to what is often a daunting process. Agencies will in turn need to work out how best to encourage more black applicants for social work posts (Selwyn et al, 2004).

Develop specific recruitment material

Recruitment packs may need to be developed specifically for particular communities, reflecting the cultural and racial background of the children who need families in that area. Feedback on this material from community leaders is likely to be of benefit.

An increasing number of families from Eastern Europe will be using services. Any family whose first language is not English should be especially sensitively welcomed. Translated recruitment material may be useful, and the use of picture-format or direct verbal contact might suit some people who have lacked formal education. These families will need to demonstrate that any child placed would not be isolated from a literate English-speaking network and that there would be effective ways for the child to access support in school and the local community.

It may be that adoption and fostering are regarded differently in different communities. It is not uncommon for BME potential carers to fear the process itself. For example, the London Borough of Ealing established a project to find out why so few African and African Caribbean people came forward to adopt. The reasons emerged as:

- housing/space concerns;
- financial concerns;
- fear of being judged and not respected/failure to understand black families/reported negative experiences;
- fear of the assessment process;
- motivation/cultural issues around discussing infertility;
- the extent to which the UK was seen as a permanent home;
- lack of awareness.

Understanding these barriers was a useful starting point for recruitment (Commission for Social Care Inspection, 2006, p 25).

Appoint recruitment "outreach workers"

Sensitive exploration of a community's fears will lead to better communication all round. Importantly, the needs of children who are waiting must be conveyed, and some agencies have appointed a key worker with responsibility for recruitment expressly for this purpose. St Francis Children's Society's Anancy Black Families Initiative in Milton Keynes, for example, employs three community outreach workers whose role is to make links with people of black and dual mixed heritage. They have developed guidance for social workers on assessing cultural competence; and they include existing adopters and carers in the professionals' planning meetings to give advice.

Make a point of welcoming older, single people

A valuable resource which can be overlooked in any ethnic group is the older, single woman who might be comfortable with the idea of permanent fostering but not adoption. It may occasionally be in a child's interest to change the plan to permanent fostering so that a particularly suitable match can happen. These women are also commonly deterred from even taking the first step because of misinformation about an age-bar.

For a very thorough exploration of the issues involved in recruiting black families, see Rule (2006).

Recruiting families for disabled children

The first assumption workers tend to make is that only people with experience of disability are appropriate to care for a disabled child. This is a huge barrier and may be ruling out sensitive and sensible people who can demonstrate in other ways that they are suitable. Although people with experience may be more confident and even more realistic than inexperienced people, a robust assessment of all families is needed – not a negative response based on untested assumptions.

The next big question for agencies recruiting families for disabled children is whether these campaigns should be specific (labelled "disability") or general, and whom to target.

Specialised "disability" recruitment campaigns

These draw in a small number of people who have particularly set out to adopt or foster a disabled child. These are often people with a disabled family member, a professional connection with disability, or a religious or ethical motivation. They may be found through:

- special schools;
- hospitals;
- short breaks schemes;
- carers' groups;

- church communities;
- political or community activist groups;
- the specialist disability press;
- other specialist publications likely to be seen by people in the caring professions, such as *Community Care*, *The Big Issue* or *The Nursing Times*.

For these people, there may be fewer stereotypes, less fear of the unknown and more confidence that they can meet the challenges. These potential carers are the easiest to attract because they are motivated, but there are relatively few of them.

For some children with very specialised needs, a particular group may suggest itself. For example, for the small number of children with a profound hearing impairment, the Deaf community would be a good starting point.

General recruitment campaigns (which include "disability")

People who have no experience of disability and little confidence that they will manage are unlikely to respond to a *specific* disabled children's campaign.

Disability in the abstract evokes images of wheelchairs, adaptations to houses, insuperable difficulties with transport, perhaps challenging behaviour – all the negatives. So a campaign that is heralded as featuring disabled children generically may not work. If, based on ignorance and fear, potential families have ruled out the possibility of taking a "disabled child" right at the beginning of the process, they never even get to know a child as an individual. We therefore need a different strategy to enable possible links to happen.

People can be drawn in through a general recruitment campaign showing a variety of children, some with visible impairments, some with none – all enjoying themselves. At the next stage they can be shown material about *all* the available children whom the agency needs to place, and at this point they might suddenly experience a connection with a child who happens to be disabled. They will have been helped to understand the impairment as just part of this child – and that they would be taking on *this* child, not "disability" in general. This approach is much more enabling for families – and much less discriminatory for children. More to the point, disabled children have been known to find families this way.

> *A participant in one of BAAF's "Opening Doors" workshops told a remarkable story. For years her team had run an annual recruitment campaign to encourage families to come forward for disabled children. The response was often discouraging, but this particular year the team were surprised and delighted by an upturn in the response. Eventually a colleague pointed to a mistake in proofreading the publicity material. They had inadvertently missed out the word "disabled" on the flyers and posters. One might have thought that the potential carers would now disappear, but no. They were shown photographs and details of the waiting children and, given the opportunity to hear more about each child's individual needs (as opposed to a generic image of a disabled child) and the supports which would be available, they felt able to make their applications and begin the home studies.*
>
> (Cousins, 2006, p 28)

Checklist for Tip 2

- Recruit only the families you need.
- Know the general profile of the agency's waiting children; show relevant images.
- Use your local consortium.
- Tailor recruitment to the needs of the children.
- Put children's needs, not adults' needs, first.
- Collaborate with other agencies in the area, and/or establish consortia.
- Try a highly focused campaign around a small cluster of children with similar needs.

Checklist (BME children)

- Appoint a good balance of black and minority ethnic staff.
- Work with the local community and use community events to publicise the need for carers.
- Invite a member of a local community group to sit on your adoption/fostering panel.
- Develop specific recruitment material, including material in common local languages.
- Run training sessions in different community languages.
- Appoint outreach workers with a recruitment role in the community.
- Make a point of welcoming older, single people.
- Find ways of connecting with people who may not be literate.
- Make sure that staff who can use community languages are available.
- Ensure that published material dispels common misperceptions, and that agency follow-up is consistent with this.

Checklist (disabled children)

- Assess families objectively for what they can do now, not only for what they have done in the past.
- Go to wherever there are people who feel comfortable with disability.
- Consider running a campaign which is not signalled as specifically to do with disabled children.
- Include disabled children among the whole range of young people in the publicity material.

TIP 3

Welcome a diverse group of people

Good practice in spreading the word about adoption and fostering and increasing the pool of carers must take account of common prejudices among both the public and social workers. In particular, attention must be paid to the untapped resources of people from marginalised groups, who must be valued objectively for what they have to offer.

Suitable families come in all shapes and sizes; many are reconstituted, with complex family relationships, step-parents, step-siblings and split households. Some households are multi-generational. Some people are in their forties and fifties. Many prospective carers already have their own children; and some have chosen not to have birth children. Increasingly, people are in unmarried partnerships or civil partnerships, both of which adoption law now recognises in England and Wales. New adoption legislation in Scotland makes a similar provision, and is due to be implemented in 2008. There are proposed changes in adoption strategy for Northern Ireland, which include extending eligibility to adopt to unmarried couples or civil partnerships. But it is unclear as yet what the final legislation will look like or when it may be implemented. There has been a long journey from the days of infertile married couples wanting to adopt babies.

Recruit from marginalised groups

Most people tend to orientate towards people who reflect their own, maybe narrow, value base or lifestyle. If the widest possible pool of carers is to be recruited for the children who need families – people who have had different life experiences and have a range of talents to offer – thinking "outside the box" is needed. Studies have made it abundantly clear that a very wide spectrum of people have proved to be successful parents. Recruitment teams must themselves come from a variety of backgrounds and must be willing to go to places where various sub-cultures congregate; they must also be willing to take advice from people who know.

One salutary lesson comes from the Commission for Social Care Inspection, which noted:

> *Only three agencies referred specifically to the recruitment of same-sex couples, three to single people and two to disabled people.*
>
> *(2006, p 26)*

This highlights the need for agencies to challenge their own prejudices and make their recruitment campaigns genuinely inclusive.

Lesbian and gay carers

Agencies are now more open to considering same-sex couples as a potentially valuable resource for children, but this "welcome" message has to a large extent not been heard by the public – it is not loud enough or not trusted. It is possible that some lesbians and gay men may doubt their own suitability to fit into the system and anticipate rejection, in which case the nature of their reception will be crucial.

With a vibrant gay community grapevine often at work, an agency cannot afford to get a reputation for being unhelpful, discriminatory or inefficient. Commentators point out that:

> *...staff members need to be comfortable working with lesbians and gay men: this includes all levels of staff – from reception to senior management.*
>
> (Mallon and Betts, 2005, p 30)

As with all "minority" or marginalised groups, targeting recruitment at the specialist press is useful. For example, *The Gay Times*, *The Pink Paper*, *Diva* and *G3* are said to attract the white middle classes, while lesbians and gay men from other classes and ethnic backgrounds are known to be more effectively reached through the mainstream press. Producing publicity material which reflects the diverse nature of prospective carers should in any case become second nature to marketing staff. It is easy to show images on buses and billboards of same-sex couples with children, and to make specific reference to welcoming lesbian and gay people. It is seen as very positive when the terms lesbian and gay are used in this forthright way: hiding behind phrases such as "welcoming people irrespective of sexuality" suggests that the agency feels uncomfortable with the issue: a powerful deterrent. In-service training suggests itself.

Single people

Single people, of whichever sexual orientation, are known to provide very good care (Owen, 1999) but may need specific encouragement to see that what they are offering is a valuable and much-needed resource. Unfortunately, they can be put off because they read children's profiles which may stipulate a two-parent family even where there is no evidence to support this so-called requirement.

Myths and difficulties need to be tackled head-on. For example, Owen found that fears about children's sensitivity to difference were unfounded: children who had been adopted by single carers felt neither unusual nor stigmatised. Many children had come from a single-parent household and thought their new family structure was quite normal. Owen uncovered many positive features about single-person adoption: consistency of parenting; intense, attachment-forming relationships; community involvement through employment. However, thought needs to be given to making single people welcome in preparation groups where the majority of participants are in couples; to ensuring that assessment does not get exclusively diverted into exploring single status at the expense of other issues; and to considering the consequences of a new adult partnership forming after the child has been placed.

The strength of myths has a profound influence on recruitment. A poll conducted by Fostering Network, described in Betts (2007, p 23), found that a quarter of people polled in Northern Ireland thought that you have to be married to foster; a quarter in Wales thought that you have to own your own home; one in three people polled in Scotland thought that foster carers were not allowed to work full-time. These misperceptions may account for the huge shortfall in foster carers, and to some extent, adopters. Agencies need to make their criteria for selection explicit. The earlier warning to dispel common myths is well grounded.

Again, positive campaign messages about the general characteristics required must be backed up by a welcoming initial response from the agency when people ring them. That first contact is crucial. If "word of mouth" is a powerful recruiter, a bad experience can be transmitted just as easily. Agencies who have particular difficulty in recruiting might benefit from an analysis of their processes. For example, if the second question asked is 'What is your husband's name?', this gives a strong message that couples are the norm. The single carers who contributed to Betts' study were a diverse group, but characterised by their maturity, determination, commitment and experience of managing difficult situations. Most of them had given a lot of thought to their application and had waited until the time was right. These are qualities to be valued.

Thankfully the number of single applicants who have had placements seems to be increasing (Adoption Register Annual Report, 2006).

Disabled adults

By law, there should be no blanket ban or generic bar to a person with an impairment becoming a carer. As with all applicants, the relevant question is 'Can this person do the task?' – or 'Can this partnership, one of whose members is disabled, do the task?'

Powerful cultural prejudices are at work throughout the adoption process which operate against disabled people (Wates, 2002). For example, there are very few positive images of disabled parents in general circulation; sex education in schools focuses on contraception for disabled young people rather than family planning; agencies running parenthood and maternity classes have traditionally paid scant attention to the accessibility of the venue; and there has been a tendency to promote the idea of "young carers" (a perspective which diminishes the disabled parents), rather than provide the necessary support to the adults themselves. In brief, society broadly does not even accept that disabled people should conceive and rear their own biological children, let alone become carers of someone else's.

Prejudice begins with the agency's often discriminatory recruitment strategy: how many posters or leaflets positively welcome disabled people as carers? For BME disabled people, the discrimination is doubled (Wates, 2000); and where those applicants are single BME women, the barriers at both the approval and matching stage can seem insurmountable.

The question of support is always raised when agencies consider disabled carers – a legitimate question for all applicants. If the disabled person is part of a couple, the able partner's contribution should not be overlooked. Often partnerships have long since worked out perfectly feasible ways of managing their life together.

Make sure that disabled adults are considered for both disabled and not-disabled children

There is also an unspoken view that disabled adults should be matched with disabled children, regardless of the objectively assessed needs of the child or capacities of the adult. Disabled adults may indeed feel that what they have learned from their particular experience of adversity could be usefully applied on behalf of a disabled child. However, they should be considered for the full range of children; indeed, the resourcefulness and determination which many disabled people demonstrate in the course of daily living are exactly the qualities needed in all adoptive parents and foster carers.

Organise anti-discrimination training for staff and panels
Oppressive values persist – perhaps most perniciously at the informal level where decision-making is less transparent. Even if approved, it is known from repeated anecdotes that disabled adults have especial difficulty in being matched with a child. Staff and panels need to be helped to confront these prejudices, which ultimately deny some children a permanent family. Social workers will need to commit themselves to making extra, proactive efforts towards a match if they are not to lose their valuable resource.

To support and encourage disabled prospective carers, disabled staff need to be visible within the agency. Many agencies not housed in new premises will also need to consider how to make their buildings fully accessible to a range of people with a variety of disabilities, and ensure that the environment also has positive images of disabled people.

Checklist for Tip 3
- Make a point of recruiting from marginalised groups: they have been largely ignored until now and may be a rich seam.
- Challenge your own prejudices: demand good supervision to help you stay objective.
- Look widely for potential carers and go to where various sub-cultures are likely to meet.
- Take advice from people who know.
- Be explicit in your campaigns, e.g. 'we welcome same-sex couples'; 'we value what single carers can offer'; 'if you are disabled we would like to hear from you'.
- Make sure all your publicity images include a variety of people.
- Ask for training on lesbian and gay fostering and adoption, and make sure this is offered across the agency and to panel.
- Check that your language on forms, posters, etc, is inclusive and that training material for groups also includes lesbian

and gay people, single carers and disabled people.
- Offer support groups for all "minority" carers who might value this.
- Make sure that disabled adults are considered for both disabled and not-disabled children.
- Organise anti-discrimination training for staff and panels.
- Employ more minority-group staff.
- Make sure your buildings are disabled-accessible.

TIP 4

Prepare and train families well

The next step in creating a pool of potential carers is to invite people into "the system", educate them about all aspects of adoption and fostering and prepare them thoroughly for this new stage of their lives. Some of the procedures described below derive from the Adoption and Children Act 2002, but also provide guidelines for good practice in permanent fostering.

Explain "the system"

Agencies are required, prior to deciding whether to issue an adoption application form, to provide written information, an invitation to an enquirers' meeting and an individual counselling interview. As with many adoption procedures, there are timescales for responding to initial enquiries: written information must be sent within five working days, and an invitation to an adoption information meeting within two months. Some form of checklist is useful to remind staff about these timescales.

The overall aim at each stage, whether adoption or fostering, is that families should understand what the task of caring for someone else's child entails, the range of complexities in looked after children's lives, and how the system works. At this point, only general information will be issued: identifying details about children will not be discussed until much later in the process.

Consider carefully before issuing an application form

As indicated earlier, in certain general circumstances it is thought to be legally possible for an agency to refuse to issue adoption application forms. In line with the National Adoption Standards described in Chapter 2, agencies are not required to accept, for example, applications from large numbers of couples who want young white babies if they (the agency) have very few young white babies to place. It can be wasteful of everyone's time and disappointing for prospective carers. It also deflects energy from finding families for the children who are likely to wait longer for a placement.

Certain criminal convictions ("specified offences") and matters of residence/domicile or being under the legal age will definitely rule out people from applying; but issues such as health, disability, weight, smoking and so on must be given individual consideration through the assessment process. To refuse to consider applications for these reasons could be interpreted as operating a "blanket ban", which is proscribed. If an agency believes it has grounds for significant concern about an individual prospective applicant's suitability, and the individual, after receiving counselling, does not accept the validity of those concerns, the agency should consider taking legal advice before refusing to issue an application form.

The four main steps once an adoption application has been accepted are: checks, preparation, assessment, and references. Checks and preparation are dealt with here, and assessment and references in Chapter 5.

Make sure that all the checks are in place

As part of its duty to check the background of a prospective adopter, the agency has to obtain the following information:

- enhanced Criminal Records Bureau (CRB) checks in England and Wales; Scotland Disclosure checks in Scotland, or POCVA checks in Northern Ireland;

- written reports of interviews with three personal referees;
- a report from the local authority in whose area the applicant lives.

The CRB check (formerly known as a police check) is a search into records about the applicant and any member of their household over the age of eighteen. A "specified offence" will rule out the person from adopting and, though covered by different regulations, from fostering also. Non-specified offences will be dealt with on a discretionary basis by the agency. Workers need to keep in mind at all times that the safety and welfare of children are paramount.

Other checks which should be in place to safeguard children are:

- employment history;
- time spent living and working abroad;
- previous partners where there has been joint parenting;
- adult children from previous relationships;
- risk assessment of household pets;
- health and safety checks (including the storage of firearms).

The best agencies have comprehensive checklists for each of these issues. The referee visits explored in Chapter 5 can be used to verify what the applicants have said about themselves and their life-style.

Plan your group preparation and training carefully

The stage of general preparation and training for prospective families is very important, and workers will need special skills in order to educate carers effectively.

Some agencies with small numbers of prospective adopters/carers may wish to join with a neighbouring authority so that their training programmes can be offered more frequently. It is not good to delay the start of home studies for the lack of available training/preparation groups. In order to include as many people as possible, the sessions must be held during what the staff might consider unsocial hours: many agencies hold groups in the evenings and some at weekends. It is not acceptable only to prepare one of the partners: parenting is a whole-family business. In the past, fathers were at risk of marginalisation where events held during working hours meant that they either lost income, or missed the training. This happens less often nowadays.

Where single prospective carers wish to bring a relative or friend to the preparation groups, this should be welcomed: you are not only preparing the carer, but their support group too.

There is a school of thought which says that if any reasonable adult is fully informed about the task, they can decide for themselves whether they can do it. During the 1980s, self-assessment (indeed *group* self-assessment) was tested as a method, but it never really entered the mainstream. What is undoubted, however, is the need to educate and prepare applicants for the very complex job ahead. Having considered all the implications, some people may decide to withdraw at this stage.

The training curriculum

The core issues to be covered by the training curriculum are prescribed by the Practice Guidance *Preparing and Assessing Prospective Adopters* (Department for Education and Skills, 2006, pp 23–24) in four parts:

- overview, assessment and decision making;
- matching, placement and adoption;
- the child;
- skills and capacities.

The publication *Preparing to Adopt* (Beesley *et al*, 2002) is an invaluable resource. These workbooks (one for applicants, one for trainers) provide a common curriculum for a UK-wide training programme so that agencies can exchange families in the knowledge that the same issues have been covered to a common standard. The curriculum covers the following subjects:

- Who are the children? Why do they need permanence?
- Child development and attachment – how children learn to feel secure.
- Overcoming the effects of neglect and abuse.
- Loving and losing, and keeping family links alive.
- Who am I? – Identity, self-esteem and resilience.
- Long-term challenges of adoption and ongoing support.
- Matching, linking and understanding the whole process.

The workbooks are designed primarily for adoption, but are useful in fostering also. The opportunity to share this learning with others in a safe group, managed by experienced social workers, gives applicants the chance to understand (generally) who the children are, the backgrounds they come from and the implications of becoming new parents. Invaluable additions to training programmes are the contributions from experienced adopters or foster carers, whose testimony is often heard in silence and not a little awe. There is nothing so powerful as hearing "from the horse's mouth" what it is like to live with a child who initially fails to attach and then, over perhaps many months or even years, gradually learns to trust the new parents.

Many applicants find that they have made an important emotional and psychological journey by the time they complete training programmes such as these – a journey that will have provided a crucial foundation for the home study and everything which follows.

Prepare families for the idea of contact

Although discussed in more detail later, contact is mentioned here because it is known to hold particular fears for adopters – more so than for foster carers. In fact, Simmonds (2001), in his analysis of the 1999 National Adoption Week campaign, found that 43 per cent of people who dropped out of the process following their initial enquiry mentioned anxiety about being able to cope with contact between the child and their birth family. Contact is indeed a difficult concept for some families to grasp: adopters are expected to "claim" children, yet accept that the child is never truly theirs.

The range of contact possibilities should be explained. Contact can mean anything from direct meetings, through telephone calls to screened letterbox arrangements. With the explosion of easy-to-use communication methods such as mobile phones, text messages, digital cameras and email, the whole idea of contact continually needs revisiting. (For a discussion of contact, see Bond (2007).)

Clarify what letterbox contact means
Letterbox contact is often misunderstood by applicants. When asked, most adopters in a particular study said that "post-box" had been discussed with them, but some thought they would be writing directly to the birth parents (Selwyn, 2005). They thought the point of letterbox contact was to meet the needs of the birth parents, but in a way that was safer than direct contact. On the whole, the adopters

liked the fact that letterbox contact:

- was anonymous;
- encouraged regular discussions;
- was a link to "a life that might have been";
- was a means of establishing direct contact later;
- meant they knew something of each other;
- meant there were benefits to the birth family and the child.

They disliked:

- delays in letters;
- the lack of clarity about rules;
- inadequate censoring;
- the idea that children might be identified through photographs;
- feeling pressured;
- the lack of reciprocity;
- unexplained changes in the pattern of correspondence.

One adopter in the study (Selwyn, 2005) said:

> *There's a lack of feedback. You put all that personal stuff in the post and it's hard to give over. We don't get any feedback that the birth parents need and want information. We need feedback otherwise we get discouraged. And when do you stop? How long does post-box go on for?*

There is a note of desperation in this quotation which is easy to understand. Nevertheless, all these issues need to be raised at the preparation stage.

Invite someone to speak who has "done it"

Throughout the process, applicants will hear a great deal about contact and it is vital that their fears should be addressed and that contact in all its forms should be clarified. Again, there is nothing more powerful in dispelling fantasies than someone who has done it – so invite a confident adopter who can describe the pitfalls of contact, how they got round them and what they have found to be the advantages.

When preparing applicants, include references to disabled children

For reasons which are elaborated upon throughout this book, disabled children are always at risk of being seen as a separate species in whom only a small minority of people are interested – but they are just displaced children who happen to have an additional difficulty. It is therefore vital to include disability issues as an integrated part of all training and preparation. If a separate "disability" session is held, it is unlikely that many will attend, almost as though people are thinking 'I don't want one of those' (whoever "those" are). It is therefore important to weave disabled children's needs into everything that is discussed so that they cannot be marginalised.

Offer specific preparation groups for "minority" applicants

It is possible that some people may feel more secure to learn about adoption and fostering in the company of people in a similar situation. Some agencies provide preparation groups for particular religious groups; and maybe offering a group for single applicants or lesbian and gay applicants would be helpful at this early stage when people's confidence is likely to be at a low ebb.

Train as a trainer

Preparing to Adopt suggests a universally valuable curriculum for preparing new carers. However, in order to make good material come alive, trainers need to be skilled and comfortable in working within an adult learning framework. Kolb's experiential learning cycle (experience, reflection, conceptualisation, experimentation – or "feeling, thinking and doing") is a helpful starting point (Kolb, 1984). Trainers will need to be able to devise learning outcomes and plan programmes; develop ground-rules and good introductions; and to hone skills in presentation, using equipment, taking feedback, co-working, troubleshooting and evaluation.

Not everyone likes performing in this way, but for social workers keen to take this on, some basic grounding in training methods is very helpful. "Training the trainers" courses are widely available.

Does training include "assessment"?

Agencies will need to be open with their applicants about the degree to which people's participation in the group setting becomes part of their overall assessment. Although adults learn best when they are relaxed and can concentrate on the content of the material, the new adoption regulations in England say that feedback to the social worker who is doing the home-study assessment is part of the process. This feedback can be a joint record by prospective carer and trainer so that areas for further exploration are identified in an open way.

Checklist for Tip 4

- Explain the "system" to enquirers.
- Make sure you know the flow-chart and timescales for the early stages of the application. Devise a checklist.
- Do not operate a "blanket ban". Consider getting legal advice before refusing to issue application forms.
- Be punctilious about all the checks and safeguards.
- Plan your group training carefully. Assemble good training materials and programmes.
- Do joint training with a neighbouring agency if this means that groups can be offered more frequently.
- Be clear with applicants about the assessment component in the training course.
- Insist that both partners attend, and make practical arrangements to enable this to happen.
- Welcome other close family members or friends if requested.
- Invite experienced carers to speak at the training course.
- Prepare families for the idea of contact.
- Particularly clarify what letterbox contact means.
- Invite someone to speak who has "done it".
- Include disability issues throughout all training sessions.
- Offer specific preparation groups for "minority" applicants.
- Ask to be sent on a "Training the Trainers" course to enhance your skills.

TIP 5

Assess applicants thoroughly

Be clear about the purpose of assessment

Assessment is designed to:

- understand the strengths and weaknesses of the applicant and to form a view about their capacity to care for a child;
- identify areas where the applicant will need further development, including (for adopters) the provision of adoption support;
- assess the stability and permanence of the relationship, where a couple are applying;
- contribute to the preparation of the final report;
- enable the assessor to make a proposal to panel about the applicant's suitability either to adopt or foster a child.

Assessment is a skilled job – it is not a case of writing down what people say and filling in forms. Assessment is also intimately connected with preparation, as applicants learn much about both themselves and "the task" through the assessment process. This goes for other family members too, who should be included where appropriate.

The assessing social worker preparing the key reports in adoption must be qualified to do so, as set out in regulations, and most fostering agencies will also wish to adhere to these requirements.

The assessment

The Prospective Adopter's Report contains the assessment, additional information from enhanced CRB or Form F and other checks, references, and feedback from the preparation groups. Reports for fostering are similar.

Get training, supervision and support in assessment

Assessment is a difficult and skilled process because assessors have to weigh everything they learn about the applicants in the context of theory, research and their own professional experience. It is made more personal because it takes place in a domestic setting where the worker is treated like a guest. Although a lot is learned by meeting people in their homes, it can lead to an unhelpful blurring of roles and even collusion. One suggestion would be for new workers to invite applicants to the office for some interviews, although this is controversial and rarely done.

During the home study it is important to convey to applicants that evidence of having overcome problems is more important than finding families without problems. Prospective carers should be helped to understand why their past experiences and current lifestyle are relevant. Social workers must discover to what extent the applicants have reflected upon and learned from these experiences: did things just happen to them or were they agents in the events? For example, the fact that applicants are already parents is not by itself evidence that they will be suitable as *adoptive* parents/carers; but showing that their own children have both emotional health and wellbeing would go some way towards demonstrating a capacity to parent an adopted child.

Use a variety of perspectives

Assessment methodologies are not prescribed, and are the subject of much discussion. Considering the following perspectives will be helpful.

- Understanding the personal qualities of the applicants.
- Evaluating the competence of the applicants to parent a vulnerable child.
- Assessing the attachment style of the prospective carers.

- Taking into account how others view the applicants (referee evaluation).
- Using evidence to support these perspectives.

Personal qualities

Little formal attention has been paid to the personal characteristics that contribute to make a successful adopter or foster carer, although common sense would suggest that these are important. Quinton (2004, p 226) supports this view:

> *The success of foster care depends heavily on the qualities of the foster carer. Some of these qualities – their commitment, "stickability"...are not normally called "skills" but are important characteristics.*

Research shows in particular that flexibility is crucial: having rigid, preconceived ideas about the "kind of child" is a negative indicator. Some of the other necessary qualities are:

- empathy;
- resilience;
- stability and reliability;
- the ability to manage change (including loss);
- being positive about difference ("live and let live");
- being able to admit the need for support and feeling comfortable with others' dependence;
- having a strong sense of personal identity (being "comfortable in one's skin");
- being able to deal with conflict constructively;
- being co-operative in dealings with others.

Many of these qualities overlap, and of course the list is not definitive.

These fundamental characteristics come from a unique combination of nature and nurture. They provide a way of understanding what an individual's default mode might be – the "type" to which they are likely to revert under stress. It is not enough to know how people respond when things are going well; there needs to be a way of predicting how they might react when the going gets tough, as it surely will. A good example of this is the driving test: it is all very well to demonstrate that you are competent to pass the test, but how do you behave when someone cuts you up on a roundabout? New children entering the family will undoubtedly cause higher stress levels than this, and applicants' likely reactions need to be understood.

In addition, assessors must consider how to evidence these qualities. This will be explored in more detail below.

Competences

If personal qualities are the building blocks of a future secure relationship between adults and child, it is also necessary to look at the here-and-now of the applicants' abilities – whether they have the skills to care for someone else's child in the best possible way. These skills are described as "competences", and are referred to in both the fostering Code of Practice (National Foster Care Association, 1999), and in the adoption Practice Guidance (Department for Education and Skills, 2006). They are grouped into five categories, each with its own detailed criteria.

- Caring for children
- Providing a safe and caring environment
- Working as part of a team
- Own development
- Adoption as a life-long process (in the case of adoption)

Applicants should be helped to look carefully at these competences so that they can really imagine what the task ahead will involve.

Attachment theory

The main attachment tool currently being developed in family-finding is the Attachment Style Interview for Adoption and Fostering (ASI-AF). This interview generates useful data relevant to family functioning. It provides a categorisation of attachment style, an assessment of the quality of the person's close relationships and an evaluation of future support needs. It also has the capacity to identify both vulnerability and resilience factors in carers. Its administration requires a four-day training course, which some agencies have provided for staff in order to use the methodology in home studies.

Look for evidence of people's qualities and skills/abilities

A crucial aspect of a rigorous assessment process is the question of evidence. Independent evidence is required not because people lie, but because self-perception may to some degree be distorted. It is preferable for a range of evidence to be supplied to support claims both about personal qualities and "competence".

For example, evidence of personal qualities can come from people who know the applicant well and from the social worker's observations during the preparation and assessment process. The applicant who is willing to change an arrangement without irritation, who keeps all their appointments, who has adjusted to domestic upheaval with equanimity, who is able to ask for help (and so on) might reasonably be regarded as showing flexibility, reliability, an ability to manage change, and the humility necessary to depend on others.

Evidence that the applicants are competent to care for children might partly be provided by an evaluation of their domestic environment such as a Health and Safety assessment – is the worker shown the garden fence, smoke alarms, seat belts, safety glass, cooker guards, catches on cupboards and so on? Other evidence might be a statement from a friend or a testimonial letter from a professional; a relevant qualification; the completion of a particular task; or interviews with other people about specific issues.

Try to remain objective: get good supervision for this

Social workers need also to be alert to the applicants' behaviour, body language and unconscious signals. If the worker feels uncomfortable, there will be a reason. There is often such fear and guilt among social workers that their own negative reaction could be coming from underlying prejudice that they fail to take their "gut feeling" seriously. Good supervision is needed to tease out the issues.

Subconscious collusion with applicants is also a risk. Social workers who assess fellow social workers and other professionals find that these are among the most difficult assessments to do objectively, primarily because the applicants may have a similar lifestyle and value-base to the assessor's. It is also worth acknowledging that many applicants, through desperation rather than dishonesty, will try to "play the system". Faced with an impending home visit, the consequences of which are hugely important, most people would make the house tidy (but not too tidy! – it must be clean, but welcoming to children) and give the "right" answers to the seemingly endless questions.

Co-working on assessments, team supervision and "second opinion" visits can all prove very helpful even to experienced social workers. Second opinion visits at the end of a home study are only strictly required in England and Wales under the 2002 Adoption and Children Act where there is cause for concern, but many agencies find them useful in other circumstances and in fostering assessments.

Look for evidence of "process"

In exploring people's histories, it is not the nature of the experiences (positive or negative) which is of relevance, but how the adult has processed them. Has the applicant avoided a fixation with the event? Is he or she able to reflect upon it, learn from it and place it in a healthy context? This relates to some degree to the attachment-style interviews discussed above. Children will inevitably trigger memories, and the applicants must be able to respond openly to the child's needs, not foreground their own unresolved issues.

Take accounts by referees very seriously

Personal referee interviews form a crucial adjunct to the assessment process. If properly conducted, they make an important contribution.

The 2002 adoption legislation (often used as a guideline in fostering) states that written references, followed by face-to-face interviews, are required from three people, not more than one of whom should be a relative. Some agencies choose to ask routinely for more than three, and more can be useful if there is concern or if specific issues need to be checked. A referee should know the applicant personally and be familiar with their home environment. Bank managers, priests and GPs are rarely used for these reasons. One of the referees should have known the person for at least five years; and where the applicants are a couple, at least two of the referees should know both the applicants well. It is preferable if the personal knowledge of the referees covers different stages of the applicants' lives, such as during young adulthood and middle age. The advantages of interviewing relatives have never been sufficiently researched: anecdotally it is known that relatives can sometimes give a brutally honest account not through malice, but through a genuine desire to protect their loved one from a course they consider ill-advised.

The subject of referees was of necessity explored in 1999 when John, a four-year-old child placed for adoption in Brighton & Hove, was killed six months after placement. (Although the adopters were originally charged with murder, the case never reached the crown court because there was no way of proving which of the adopters, if either, inflicted the blows that killed the child.) The enquiry into John's death revealed concern about the impartiality of the adopters' referees, and recommended that applicants should supply the names of at least six referees, from which list the social worker would choose three to interview. It is not known to what extent agencies have followed this advice. Alyson Leslie, who conducted the Part 8 Review, wrote:

> *...no test is too rigorous and no questioning too intrusive, where the credibility, honesty and reliability of individuals who wish to become adopters are concerned.*
>
> *(Leslie, 2001, p 29)*

Although the content of the referee interview is not shared with the prospective carers, should anything very serious emerge, the social worker cannot give an absolute guarantee of confidentiality.

Devise a leaflet for referees
An agency leaflet for applicants to show to prospective referees is helpful. It should include information about the task of

adoption/fostering so that the referee is fully prepared for the kind of issues which will be discussed. It should also explain that agreeing to be a referee involves a serious undertaking to help establish whether the family in question could provide a safe and caring environment for a child. The appointment letter setting up the interview with referees should reiterate these points.

Interview former partners

Following the death of the child in Brighton & Hove, it is now recommended (Department for Education and Skills, 2006, p 16) that ex-partners are interviewed if they have jointly parented. Had the male adopter's former wives been interviewed (he had been married twice before), suspicions would have been aroused about his suitability as a parent.

It is known that some applicants will not readily agree to this, seeing it as too intrusive. Occasionally they will cite fear of violence, in which case divorce papers can be requested which would corroborate this. Concerns about a biased and vindictive account following a "messy" divorce is often the basis for the initial refusal. The applicant may need to be reassured that one divergent account will be unlikely to negate other positive references.

Check with other people
Adult children

It is usual to interview any adult children who still live with or near the applicants, and those who have a very close relationship with the household. It would be reasonable to assume that their attitude to adoption or fostering will be important in the years to come. Certainly adult children of a previous marriage should be interviewed.

Children's school

Much can often be learned by a conversation with the school head or classroom teacher for any existing children in the family. As with other checks, the applicant's permission must be sought.

Employer

Checks should be carried out with the prospective carer's current employer that will verify employment dates, and whether there have been any disputes or disciplinary proceedings. Fears that contacting an employer may jeopardise employment prospects are largely unfounded, though court cases are occasionally reported where someone has been unfairly dismissed because of impending child-care commitments. Previous employers may also be approached, and always where the employment has involved the care of children.

The Department for Education and Skills Practice Guidance, *Preparing and Assessing Prospective Adopters* (2006), is helpful when thinking about this whole issue of references.

In finalising the report, don't restrict the prospective adopter's approval status

Families coming to adoption panels for approval are not obliged to say what kind of child they would like – a label which used to become part of their post-approval identity and all too often reduced the opportunities for placement. This was (and perhaps still is) commonly misunderstood to be required by law. For example, when an agency approved a family to adopt 'one female child aged 4–6', this label became (erroneously) part of their approval status and then limited their potential response to, say, a seven-year-old boy seen in *Be My Parent*. The Adoption and Children Act 2002 is quite clear that people are simply either approved or not, but the panel may express an opinion about what kind of child may be most suitable. It is understood that this practice is quite common. Fostering panels have always been required to recommend the "kind of child" when approving carers, and this becomes part of the foster carer's approval status.

Remember that you may recommend that the applicants should not be approved as carers.

The social worker's role in assessment is not that of advocate; it is not to get the applicants through panel but to present them dispassionately. It is always possible that the assessing social worker might finally not recommend the person/couple as carers – and the panel (and the agency decision-maker) will have to take a view. As with any recommendation, a clear argument and supporting evidence will be required.

Prepare well for panel

The report on the prospective carers is presented to the panel for a recommendation to the agency; the agency decision-maker is responsible for the final decision. There are timescales governing the communication of the decision to prospective adopters.

Panels are statutory bodies independent of the agency, which perform a quality control function over key aspects of the agency's work. Different legislation covers adoption panels and fostering panels, but where specific regulations are absent, good practice from one arena usually carries over to the other.

The panel will expect high quality material which is as complete and accurate as possible. This does not always mean lengthy: the best home study reports contain all the crucial information, but are succinct and analytical. For this reason, staff would be well advised to check that their material is of a good standard and has been signed off by a manager. Their presentation to the panel should be objective: as has been said elsewhere, the social worker is not the family's advocate, and should not be trying to get them through panel at all costs.

The Independent Review Mechanism (IRM)

Social workers need to be aware that if an agency proposes to refuse approval to adopters in England, the applicants have the right to apply to the IRM. As the name suggests, this is an independent process, set up by the Government, which reviews the case de novo and makes a further recommendation to the agency. It is not a higher appeals procedure, and the final decision still rests with the agency. Prospective adopters only have recourse to the IRM once their application has been accepted by the agency. If, following the panel's consideration of either a full or a "brief" report, the applicants are dissatisfied with the agency's proposed decision, they may choose either to apply to the IRM or to make representations to the agency, but not both.

The IRM can only consider the approval of adopters, not a proposed match. The IRM does not yet apply to fostering, but this is under active consideration.

Checklist for Tip 5

- As a team exercise, try constructing a "job description" of adoption or fostering – i.e. what is the task?
- Ask for specialised training in assessment – this is a very highly skilled task.
- Use a variety of perspectives: look for personal qualities as well as "competence"; and evidence of "process".
- Suggest additional training in ASI-AF.
- Get good supervision during assessments. Team supervision can be a learning opportunity for everyone and can be very supportive.
- Help the applicants to provide a range of evidence of their qualities and skills.
- Ask for a range of referees who have known each applicant well for a long time, and at different points in their past.
- Take your referee interviews very seriously: they are a particularly rich source of evidence.
- Provide a leaflet for referees to ensure they understand the importance of their contribution and that your interview will be rigorous.
- Interview significant former partners and adult children of former relationships.
- Check with a variety of other people if necessary.
- Make sure you don't restrict the adopter's approval status.
- Remember that you may recommend that the applicants should not be approved as carers.
- Prepare well for panel.

TIP 6

Know the child

Having explored how to encourage a wide range of potential families to come forward, it is now time to look more closely at the other half of the equation: how children are to be understood, described and prepared for the family-finding process. To "know the child" should be the central tenet of any work with children and families. It is also a key "tip" in the companion volume to this one, *Ten Top Tips for Placing Children in Permanent Families*.

Build your direct work skills

Sadly, with some notable exceptions, communicating effectively with children in order to know them inside out is virtually a lost art. Social workers have become case-managers rather than communicators and relationship-builders. Visits to McDonalds are still seen as the aspirational model for work with children, but face-to-face interviews with young people over chicken nuggets is a blunt instrument. Surely there are so many more creative ways to develop a relationship with a child, and new tools which can be explored?

The word "working" with children is a cold and barren term. The intention should be to help a child to understand his/her situation, to adjust the misperceptions which come from poor early experiences, to enhance self-esteem and to support the child towards a positive future. These life-changing shifts only come about through sharing a variety of experiences in the context of a warm, reliable and enjoyable relationship. Most importantly of all, in terms of family-finding, only a relationship of this breadth and depth will give the worker the vital, full and rounded picture of the child on which to build the family-finding efforts. There is considerable risk in matching a child who is an unknown quantity with a new family.

The following tasks which have to be accomplished with children via this special relationship all go hand in hand.

- Preparation (where possible) for leaving home and becoming "looked after".
- Ongoing life-story work.
- Assessment of the child.
- Future planning/preparation for the move to permanent care.

Family finding cannot begin until all these elements are in place.

A new collection, *Direct Work: Social work with children and young people in care* (Luckock and Lefevre, 2008) offers a range of perspectives on engaging in direct work with children and young people, and stresses the need to listen to and engage and communicate with the child.

Begin life story work as early as possible

> *I don't really understand much about my parents until I read that book and I've found it helpful to understand about them and what they like to do and...how they lived and everything.*
>
> (Adopted child, quoted in Thomas, 1999, p 86)

No child should enter the looked after system without someone spending time to ensure that they have a clear understanding of their situation – why they are there, what is happening to their family and what may happen next. Crucially, a child must be relieved of the burden of believing it is their fault. This process must continue throughout their life in foster care or residential care and will often continue to be appropriate when the child is placed in a permanent family. Consolidating the child's understanding will also involve creating a tangible record in the form of a memory box, a life story book and, ideally, a short film.

Life story tools

Life story work is a process, not just a written record or photograph album. It is sensitive, highly skilled and painful work – often painful for the social worker as well as the child because it can evoke hidden sadness and a dreadful sense of failure. Social workers want to make things better for children and find it distressing when they are unable to comfort the child, or provide hope and certainty.

There are a variety of valuable tools on hand to help with life story work. Ryan and Walker's book (revised 2007) is a long-standing favourite with social workers. It describes the why, who and how of life story work in great detail. Chapter 6 of Cousins (2006) draws attention to the need to communicate with disabled children, and gives an overview of non-verbal systems and a communication toolkit. *Life Story Work* (Shah and Argent, 2006) is a guide for children and young people.

In My Shoes

One of the most engaging methods to be developed in recent years is *In My Shoes*, a computer-interactive programme which enables worker and child to explore together important events and relationships in the child's life. It can be used in discussing life story material, and for helping a young person to express wishes and feelings.

The programme, organised in a series of modules, provides a structured interview with lively scenes covering everyday domestic, school and other situations. These invite the child to identify people, settings and somatic experiences, and to choose associated feelings – mainly through clicking a mouse and adding faces which express a wide choice of emotions. The scene is then ripe for discussion, the computer screen providing an unthreatening external focus for worker and child.

The use of *In My Shoes* is restricted to practitioners who have attended a two-day training course based on an action-learning approach (Calam *et al*, 2005).

Find the time!

None of these practical suggestions is of any use unless time (and training) is allocated to this often difficult task of helping children to understand their past and current circumstances.

Assess the child thoroughly

Involving the child in the next step – planning the future – is both desirable and required by law.

Planning for any child can only ethically take place when that child is thoroughly known to the social worker. Comprehensive assessment is the cornerstone, but skills tend to be lacking (Social Care Institute for Excellence, 2006), and the time devoted to this, patchy. It is a sad consequence of the endemic staff shortages and high turnover in some agencies that, all too frequently, looked after children are passed from one social worker to another. In some cases, no one really knows the child or has responsibility long enough to support them through the family-finding process to placement. Thus a system which should act as a good parent ends up as untrustworthy and, in the worst cases, abusive. The White Paper, *Care Matters*, recognises the need to 'transform the lives of children and young people in care'(2007).

Take particular care with disabled children

The addition of a disability can make assessment even more complex and in 2000 the Department of Health raised serious concerns about the quality of assessments of disabled children. Learning disability and communication impairments are acknowledged to be challenging for professionals. But how can anyone plan for a child unless they know them? Workers must be able to "read the child" and make some sense of what they are reading. Specialist workers with expertise in a variety of communication methods need to be on hand, preferably as the disabled child's key worker or, failing that, in a support role.

In assessing any child or young person, a wide variety of information is needed, including a full history of their early experiences, separations and losses. The best assessments go right back to pre-birth factors. Argent's checklist (1996, p 2) is really helpful.

- Discuss with the child's parents.
- Get up-to-date medical reports from the GP, health visitor, any

specialist, and the agency medical adviser.
- Get reports from school and educational psychologist, and a copy of the statement of special needs or record of needs.
- Get reports from therapists: speech, art, play, physio and so on.
- Discuss with other key professionals.
- Get a detailed history of family background, including medical history.
- Assemble photographs of the child, their family and previous carers.
- Fill out the life-story with memories by family and carers.
- Write an account of the work done to help the child to understand their situation and what is planned.
- Ask the current carer to write or audio-record a 'day in the life of the child'.
- Investigate significant people in the child's life in order to plan contact both short- and long-term; and assess whether the parents are likely to be able to sustain this.
- Describe the child's ability to attach and their need to regress; their experience of separation and loss and the degree of institutionalisation.
- Collate any information about current programmes of care and/or behaviour management.
- Identify what financial support is available (it is three times more expensive to bring up a disabled child).

All the above apply equally to children who are not disabled.

Weigh up all the factors

The presence of multiple factors can lead to a false understanding of the child. Social workers need basic grounding in the competing effects of:

- learned behaviour;
- trauma;
- dysfunctional attachment;
- loss and grief;
- impairment;
- illness.

The interaction between these components makes a firm assessment extremely difficult to reach. Is a child's bedwetting the result of traumatic fear, medical/physiological difficulties, or the outcome of previous sexual abuse? Is the child who constantly breaks things in a state of perpetual stress arousal; or do they have a condition such as cerebral palsy or dyspraxia?

Hold a Child Appreciation Day (CAD) for each child

Some agencies are investing in a Child Appreciation Day, a whole-day meeting which provides the opportunity to build a full understanding of the child so that future planning is well founded. A CAD could be held at one of several valuable points:

- as a type of Family Group Conference, to (hopefully) place the child within the wider family or community network;
- to inform the family-finding process where placement outside the original family becomes the plan, by helping to construct a complete picture of the child;
- to prepare an identified family for placement, before introductions begin.

In some respects, there are similarities between CADs and disruption meetings.

The CAD is attended by as many people as possible who know the child. They are present for at least part of the day in order to make their own contribution: past and present carers; social workers (particularly those who have worked with the birth family); perhaps a teacher, paediatrician, legal adviser, therapist, health visitor, school dinner supervisor, and so on. An independent chairperson helps participants to develop an all-important chronology and flow-chart of the child's experiences from pre-birth to the present day. The visual impact of a flow-chart where a child has had several moves in a short life cannot be overstated: it provides a key means of understanding the child's experiences of loss and dislocated attachments. Patterns and new understandings emerge which then form a sound basis either for featuring the real child, for future planning or for re-parenting, depending upon the prime purpose of the meeting. Flow-charts have also proved useful in helping judges and solicitors to appreciate the child's experiences.

Checklist for Tip 6

- Build your skills in direct work. Ask for further training.
- Begin life story work as early as possible.
- Share ideas with colleagues about what contributes to making a good relationship with a child.
- Get to know the child thoroughly.
- Ask for training in life story work, communicating with children and specialist programmes such as *In My Shoes*.
- Involve the child.
- Identify workers who have specialist skills in communicating with learning-disabled and communication-impaired children.
- Gather a very wide range of information about the child: weigh up all the factors.
- Hold a Child Appreciation Day for each child.
- Practise creating flow-charts for children on your case-load. Use them widely to impress upon everyone the child's life experiences.
- Make time!

TIP 7

Make realistic plans for each child

Remember non-looked after children

In considering adoption and fostering planning for children, there is at least one group of children, repeatedly forgotten, who should be mentioned first. These are the children in special boarding schools who are outside the review system.

For some of these children, whose parents place them residentially and rarely visit, all sense of belonging to a family can gradually be lost. These children are mostly either significantly impaired or have major behavioural disorders, and the specialist facility is likely to be far from home, and expensive and inconvenient to reach. Children in entirely educational settings are only peripherally known to social services, and there is no independent review system to monitor their welfare.

The care system should be making attempts either to support the birth family, or to make alternative arrangements through permanent fostering or adoption. Staff on Children's Disability Teams who are likely to be working with the family must be vigilant, and robust in resisting collusion with parents against the interests of children. One little boy with significant autistic features was placed in a 48-week special school some distance from home, and then sent by his parents to a Health Authority respite unit for three of the four holiday weeks (again, no LAC reviews). He had scarcely any sense of family life at all. Jenny Morris has written powerfully on this subject (1995, 1998).

Looked after children

On a happier note, planning for looked after children follows a more secure path. For adoption, the legislation and guidance details exactly what should happen within certain timescales.

Some of the key issues in planning for a child are:

- the route to permanence: adoption, permanent fostering or special guardianship;
- placement together with, or apart from, siblings;
- ethnic matching;
- broad decisions about contact;
- geographical location.

These are likely to be the central concerns in planning for any individual child; other important matters will come into play if a particular family is under consideration, and are discussed in Chapter 10.

Keep an open mind on the best route to permanence for each child: an adoption plan may not secure permanence

When permanence outside the birth family is needed, adoption is usually the preferred route, particularly for young children, and there is good research evidence to support this. But many factors come into play.

Agencies are required to do all they can to minimise the time-gap between leaving the birth family and placement in a permanent new family. There are many factors which contribute to delay – staff shortages, court timetables, over-zealous additional assessments and so on – and unfortunately the requirement "adoption" can itself cause delay in achieving permanence.

It is ironic that the very concept (adoption) which is so celebrated as being in children's best interests can become an albatross around a child's neck. This arises from the reluctance of some potential families who have every intention of offering a lifetime's commitment, to take the plunge into adoption straight away. While it is important to emphasise adoption support and to encourage adoption, some children with very complex needs may never find a permanent family on this basis. Were the plan to be *either* adoption or fostering, at least families who are interested could enter a discussion process, may become convinced that adoption support would be reliably delivered or, failing that, take the child on a permanent fostering basis with the intention of moving into adoption should it feel right at some future point. There used to be a pathway called "fostering with a view to adoption" which, perhaps because of the uncertainties it represented, fell from favour but which deserves revisiting. For some children, the permanent fostering option must be considered; otherwise, ironically, the child will be in permanent limbo. The preference by some female prospective carers from black and minority ethnic groups for offering fostering over adoption was mentioned earlier.

It is possible that agencies which operate "adoption and permanence" panels may offer more opportunities for flexibility in planning.

Consider special guardianship as a valuable route to permanence for a wide range of children

Special guardianship is described in some detail in the introduction to this book. It is not yet known to what extent special guardianship will become the route of choice for some children, though the figures show that in its first year, 740 special guardianship orders (SGOs) were granted. Detailed data on the percentage of SGOs made *outside* the kinship network are currently not available.

Siblings: placement together or apart?

As a general rule, placing siblings together is a good maxim, and prospective carers who show an interest in this should be encouraged and supported. McFadden (2004) has identified that the sibling bond is:

- a strong emotional connection;
- dependent upon physical and emotional access to each other;
- a tie that unites children; closest when siblings are close in age;
- a shared history;
- the longest lasting and most enduring bond over the child's lifespan;

- a primary source of the child's identity;
- one of the most important ways a child learns about relationships.

The sibling bond is especially strong when siblings are neglected by parents and either an older sibling becomes the caregiver, or when the children mutually depend upon each other to get their needs met.

McFadden claims that when siblings are separated:

- they become depressed, and experience a loss of self;
- they blame their earlier "bad thoughts" (natural sibling rivalry/ambivalence) as the cause of the separation;
- they lose their shared history, their sense of self-worth and their future relationship.

The reasons for keeping siblings together are difficult to refute. Moreover, placing them together provides a protective factor for the success and stability of the placement. According to Rushton *et al* (2001), the single placement of a child who has siblings tends to have a poor outcome. A contra-indication to placing siblings together would be where one sibling has been extremely abusive to the other.

The aim of keeping children together is laudable, but not without its difficulties. This is especially so where there are several children, when new babies in the birth family keep coming along, or where one child has a significant impairment. There is evidence that disabled children are more likely than others to be separated from their not-disabled siblings, as this is believed to give the other children a better chance to join a permanent family. Placement together is more common where the other sibling is also disabled.

Readers will find the practice guide *Together or Apart* (Lord and Borthwick, 2001) very helpful.

Try to keep separated siblings in contact with each other
Although undesirable in principle, having separate adoptive families for siblings with complex needs can at least increase the chances of permanence for all the children. In these cases, it is vital that the children can maintain their relationships as they grow up.

Make every effort to find ethnically-matched families for children

Planning for a child must give due consideration to the child's "race", religion, language and culture. This has been explored in very helpful detail by Rule (2006), who argues forcefully that black, Asian and mixed-heritage children's identity is particularly vulnerable for those who are in the looked after system. These BME children and young people need the protection afforded by a family of similar culture and ethnicity in order to learn how to combat racism and to feel self-worth. Indeed, this value is now enshrined in standards and legislation across the UK. Recruiting and supporting BME families is the key.

As suggested earlier, having a wide choice of temporary foster carers would ensure that children can live right from the start with an ethnically matched family. This will be a positive factor should permanence with the same family eventually be considered.

Always consider post-placement contact issues

Since the mid 1980s, one of the biggest issues in adoption planning for children has been contact. Originally described in its most extreme form, "open adoption", this has now become a more nuanced idea of "openness", which encompasses an attitude and activities centred around preserving a sense of continuity for the child.

The following quotation from a young person underlines the value of contact:

> *I wish I knew if my older brothers who went into foster care are OK. They should be taking their GCSEs now...I really want to know if they are OK.*
>
> *Brendan was always so good to me; he used to pull funny faces and swing me to make me laugh. I wonder if he's going to college or got a job?*
>
> *At night I imagine he might be dead, then I pull the*

> *covers over my head and silently sob so no one hears me.*
>
> *(Oakwater, 2003, p 35)*

The importance of contact is reinforced by official sources.

> *Contacts, however occasional, may continue to have a value for the child even when there is no question of returning to his family. These contacts can keep alive for a child a sense of his origins and may keep open options for family relationships in later life.*
>
> *(Department of Health, 1991, pp 63–64)*

Broad decisions about the child's contact needs are now built into the planning process. Where things go smoothly, contact will:

- help the child to have a realistic understanding of his or her past;
- promote a sense of continuity;
- reassure the child about the well-being of the birth family;
- strengthen links with his or her heritage;
- create the possibility of maintaining communication into adulthood.

Devise clear guidelines for contact

The optimum conditions for healthy contact of whatever kind are where the agency has clear policies and procedures; makes clear agreements based on professional assessment; monitors the individual situation appropriately; and ensures that all parties are supported throughout the young person's childhood.

Support all parties
Birth parents

Where birth parents are helped to work co-operatively with the agency and either directly or indirectly with the carers, contact can be beneficial for them too. They will be kept informed about the child's development and may be able to express views about important plans. Crucially, they will know that the child has a realistic understanding of why they could not live at home. However, Selwyn (2005) found that birth parents did not fully grasp how letterbox contact would work, and this should be addressed. In some situations, of course, no form of contact can be allowed.

Adopters

For contact to work for a child's benefit, adopters and permanent carers must have an open, flexible attitude, feel positive about the birth parents, be confident that, as adopters, they are entitled to claim the child while affirming his or her past, and feel supported by the agency. Ongoing knowledge about the birth family can be helpful to carers when they explore the child's past with them.

As discussed earlier, it is very important that during early preparation and training, adopters in particular are helped to examine contact in some depth so that they become more confident. One of the fears expressed by social workers is that adopters may not follow through on their promises.

Don't underestimate the complexities of letterbox contact

In planning contact for children, letterbox arrangements are turning out to be by far the most common arrangement, providing the facility for adopters and children to receive information at agreed intervals about the birth family, and vice-versa, through an intermediary. Identifying details are removed, but the desire to know how the other party is faring is satisfied. Often erroneously believed to be the simplest form of contact to manage, letterbox arrangements are in fact proving complex for all participants and it is difficult for agencies to enforce reciprocation between parties.

Keep an open mind on contact

In general, the long-term value of contact is still being researched, and new adoption legislation is neither for nor against it. Studies are emerging which point to the quality rather than the amount of contact being paramount, and to the risks where domestic violence has been a family feature. Learning-disabled children may have different requirements, underlining the fact that each child's needs must be individually assessed.

High levels of contact, and particularly direct contact with birth parents, can deter expressions of interest from prospective families. Planning appropriate levels of contact is a delicate balancing act where children must be at the centre of decision-making.

In family-finding, think about geographical location

There are normally only two reasons why the geographical location of a permanent new family may be an immovable item in the child's plan. Firstly, safety: for some children whose parents profoundly disagree with the adoption or permanence plan and are known to be potentially violent or disruptive, the child's future whereabouts must be protected at all costs. Placing at a considerable distance does not guarantee safety, but at least minimises the risk.

Conversely, for some children, placing them in their familiar locality is not just desirable but essential: a particularly strong relationship may need nurturing, or it may be in the child's interests that a school placement should be maintained, over and above other considerations.

Avoid rigid prescriptions about "what kind of family"

At the planning stage for an individual child, if there are likely to be very few prospective carers coming forward, it is damaging to draw up a detailed specification of the ideal family required: this could blight the family-finding plan from the beginning. Sometimes, aspects of the specification are based not on evidence, but on nothing more than the worker's personal preference.

In a small piece of research on the family-finding attempts for 18 profoundly disabled children (Cousins, 2006), one child's profile in *Be My Parent* stipulated the need for 'a black two-parent adoptive family where she would be the youngest child'. Eighteen months later, this child still had no placement (indeed, had attracted no responses at all), yet the agency was adamant that, with the exception of a change of plan from adoption to fostering, the existing requirements should remain in the profile. This inflexible approach may have denied this child a family, particularly as research shows that many black people who apply are single women. The agency was by now considering residential provision with education; the child was aged six.

Examples of rigid prescriptions are:

- that the child must be the youngest;
- that a two-parent family is required;
- that the family should already have experience of raising children;
- that, in the case of a disabled child, the family should have experience of disability;
- that a lively, energetic family is needed (which appears to rule out disabled adults).

These matters will be looked at more closely in Chapter 10.

Checklist for Tip 7

- **Remember non-looked after children: they may be lost in the system.**
- **Consider whether permanence could more quickly and reliably be achieved through permanent fostering rather than adoption.**
- **Consider special guardianship as a route to permanence.**
- **Make every effort to place siblings together.**
- **Try hard to keep separated siblings in contact with each other.**
- **Make every effort to find ethnically-matched families for children.**
- **Always consider contact issues, but keep an open mind.**
- **Devise clear agency guidelines on post-placement contact.**
- **Support all parties in contact.**
- **Don't under-estimate the complexities of letterbox contact.**
- **Think about geographical location.**
- **Consider very carefully which prerequisites for a child's prospective family are absolutely essential – and can be evidenced.**
- **Even then, during the first phase of featuring a hard-to-place child, only limit the "kind of family" where absolutely necessary. The time to be selective is if you have a choice.**

TIP 8

Produce high quality material about the child

This chapter deals not with general recruitment of families and general preparation and training, but with the very specific family-search for each child.

The child's profile, photographs and video/DVD which are used to feature the child in family-finding publicity must all be of the highest quality. Note that the word "feature" is used rather than "advertise": "feature" is seen as more respectful and with fewer commercial connotations.

Whether a child eventually gets a permanent family will depend upon several things.

- The social worker's commitment
- Agency structure
- How well the social worker knows the child
- The child's involvement
- The quality of the profile

- The quality of photographs and video/DVD material
- Where the child is featured
- Luck

Luck is outside social workers' control, but hard work and imagination can be put into all the other elements. The first six of these issues are considered here and "where the child is featured" in the next chapter.

Get good supervision: your commitment needs to be supported

There is no doubt that finding a really suitable placement for a child is one of the most satisfying tasks in all social work. Conversely, if it seems not to be happening, it is one of the most distressing. During this process, workers need supportive and challenging supervision to keep them optimistic and energised. Child-care workers particularly need support in how to manage their visits when they have no news to tell a child who is waiting for a family: their guilt will be enormous and demoralising. They may find they are avoiding the child, which increases the young person's sense of loss and abandonment. Each child needs a dedicated champion who will not rest until a suitable placement is found.

Reconsider your agency structure

It is likely that the actual structure of the agency may work against successful family-finding. From talking to both child-care workers and family-finding staff, it is apparent that in agencies where generic child-care workers are responsible for the crucial early stages of the process, such as writing the Child's Permanence Report or Form E and profile, their other responsibilities with emergency child protection can divert them from this work.

In agencies which hand over all aspects of the child's case to a family-finding team after the permanence decision has been made, a more consistent focus on the child and their permanence needs can be ensured, though the family finder will not know the birth family to the same extent.

Some agencies pass the family-finding function to the worker who supervises the child's foster carer. If this worker visits out of school hours, he or she may know the child quite well in the foster home, and may know the birth family also.

No system is perfect, because where different workers become involved at different stages, the child must endure further disrupted relationships. Whoever takes over responsibility must be able to devote absolute commitment to the permanence process on behalf of the child.

Get to know the child really well

The way a child is portrayed in publicity material can make the difference between success and failure in family-finding. There are estimated to be over 4,000 children waiting for permanent families, and what is needed is the quickest and best match possible for each child.

No profile can be written without a real knowledge of the child, based on the checklist of assessment issues discussed above. A misleading representation can lead to a placement disruption because the match was based on false information. And mistaken identity also contributes to children never being placed – the child who was wrongly thought to have learning difficulties; the child whom a psychologist found could concentrate for a whole hour – previously described as having "minimal attention-span". And what a shame if a match is overlooked because a specific talent has gone unrecognised – the child who was discovered too late to have an innate musical ability but was placed in a non-musical family. Occasionally a too-rosy picture is painted in order to get the child placed at all costs: a dangerous practice.

As discussed earlier, this means that the social worker responsible for family-finding must know the child extremely well, including having all the background and family history, and have an empathetic appreciation of the child's experiences to date. If the social worker has taken over the case from a colleague, time must be allocated to read all the files.

Involve the child

It is required by law, and basic good practice, to ensure that the child's views are represented throughout the whole process of planning, and to enable the young person to contribute to writing their profile for family-finding purposes.

Extra skill is needed with children who have learning or communication difficulties, but their input is indispensable. Age-appropriate ways to include as many children as possible in representing themselves must be developed, using a variety of media – signs and symbols, computer programmes, videos, audio-technology, photographs and so on. Two good aids are the NSPCC training video and communication handbook, *Two-Way Street* (NSPCC, 2001) and the *In My Shoes* computer-assisted interview programme (Calam *et al*, 2005) mentioned elsewhere. These recommendations for imaginative profiling apply to all children, not only those with complex backgrounds or impairments.

Write good, individual profiles

Profiles of children are the lynch-pin of the whole family-finding process. These profiles can be featured in newspapers such as *Be My Parent* and the magazine *Children Who Wait*, on the web in *Be My Parent online*, and circulated to consortia members. For some children, the profile will make the difference between having a family and having no family.

Firstly, it must be ensured that as well as attracting prospective families, nobody with potential is ruled out. The messages in Chapter 7 are vital here: when writing a child's profile, never include a prescription for "family wanted" which contains anything you might be willing to negotiate about – for example, issues like the child's position in the new family, the need for a two-parent family, that the family should already have child-care experience, and so on. The more complex the child's needs, the more flexible you may have to be. Even compromising on a close ethnic match may ultimately be necessary.

The power of the profile

It takes only a very few seconds for someone (a social worker, but particularly a prospective carer) to scan and reject the details about a child, or alternatively to make a connection. If that vital link happens, the profile will be combed for its hidden nuances. Ensuring that a profile is both irresistible and robust is a massive responsibility for the writer. One social worker per team could perhaps seek training and then specialise in this skill in order to advise and guide less experienced colleagues.

Same but different

Most people, if asked to describe themselves, would neither want to be seen as the same as everyone else, nor noticeably different – they would probably opt for coming across as an everyday person with some interesting aspects. Similarly, in writing profiles of children, the skill is to combine the ordinary with the special. Conveying the essence of the child in a succinct way should be at the heart of the process.

Avoid clichés

Bland clichés are anathema. Too many profiles describe the child as having 'a smile which lights up her face' or 'a mischievous grin' or as being 'active, bubbly and affectionate', with the result that the children all tend to sound the same.

Avoid jargon

The other problem is the use of jargon. Normal people do not talk about 'making good attachments' or 'having contact with siblings' or 'reaching developmental milestones' or 'achieving our potential'. We say 'having close relationships', 'staying in touch with his brother and sister', 'doing well' or 'making the most of ourselves'. The more formulaic the description, the more wooden the child sounds.

Convey the real child

The best profiles provide a deeply individual, positive but realistic, up-to-date description, which includes *what it is which someone really likes about this child*. The child's view of himself or herself, their wants and needs, and the foster carer's own words are very important and will bring the profile to life. The following quotations make the point: firstly Douglas himself, who worries that 'there are no new mums and dads left'; then his foster carer, who says:

> *Douglas is a human noise machine. From the moment he wakes he is laughing, singing, talking, whistling.*

Suddenly Douglas is a real child.

Include the *effects* of adversity, not the trauma itself

Many children have experienced trauma which of course cannot be described in a profile – but reference to the *effects* of the trauma may be helpful for potential families to understand. For example: Jane bites her nails to the quick; Joel is very restless at night; Jamal is afraid of men; Jessie hides food under her bed.

Avoid complicated medical terms

These can be daunting, whereas giving a simple explanation or conveying the *effect* of the condition is clearer. For example, it is easier to picture a child who will 'test your patience because he has enormous energy and repeats the same action over and over again to see if he gets a response' – than a child who has 'an autistic spectrum disorder'.

Avoid stereotyping disabled children

Disabled children in particular are at risk of being stereotyped as needing pity, a cure, rescue or protection; or as being brave, especially sweet, pathetic, extra-special, rewarding or very affectionate. But they must also be allowed to be moody, sensitive, awkward, funny, selfish, unresponsive, mischievous, happy, clinging, gentle and troubled, if that is the reality.

Say what the child can do in an ordinary family environment

For disabled children, what the child *can do* as well as *can't do* in an ordinary family environment must be described in order to curb fantasy and provide a realistic image. Any honest description which gets away from the stereotype of insuperable difficulties will be helpful.

- This child can live in an ordinary house in spite of some mobility difficulties.
- This child's foster carers have found it easy to manage the feeding tube.
- This child is learning really well how to use the necessary creams and lotions for his eczema.

Don't waste words

Saying that the desired family 'must be patient, tolerant, child-centred and able to set clear boundaries' is unnecessary. Surely all families need to have these qualities?

Keep the profile up to date

An out-of-date profile damages the child's chances of a family. Particularly for very young or disabled children, things may change quite quickly.

With the advent of services such as *Be My Parent online* (www.bemyparent.org.uk), the possibilities are limitless for including engaging anecdotes, drawings and video-clips. All these features will contribute to an individualised description of the child.

Make sure that photographs are of very high quality

Photographs are extremely powerful. It is probably not an exaggeration to say that the right photograph can make or break a child's chances of finding a family.

> *Ask any adoption recruiter about an effective way to reach families and he or she will likely say that families need to see the children before they will become interested in adopting.*
>
> *(National Adoption Day, 2005, p 13)*

A subscriber survey conducted by *Be My Parent* (2004) showed that 82 per cent of respondents said that the photographs of the children were important when deciding whether to make an enquiry about a child, and a quarter said it made a big difference: 'It is harder to connect with a child if the quality of the photograph is bad.' The placement system cannot afford to lose any prospective carers.

Social workers need to consider whether the photograph conveys an accurate "message" about the child, as different people will find different characteristics appealing.

> *Attraction to a mentally handicapped child's photograph was rarely associated with a child's good looks...The first impression of some adoptive parents was that their child was ugly. They received an unspoken message from the child's picture which was associated with the child's forlorn state and special need for parents.*
>
> *(Macaskill, 1985, p 98)*

Photographs are so powerful that experts should ideally be involved. If this is not possible, *Be My Parent's* digital photography guide, available at www.bemyparent.org.uk, may be helpful. A poor image is a lost opportunity and it is arrogant to think that an amateur pointing a camera at a child will necessarily do the trick – especially tempting with the advent of easy-to-use digital cameras. The expertise of other professionals must be recognised if children's best interests are to be promoted.

But professionals must be given the right brief. There are far too many studio shots of children (like the traditional solemn school or passport photo) which are so formulaic that all individuality is ironed out.

> *A professional photographer decided to expand her family by adopting a child from foster care. She was taken aback by the lifeless "mug shots" that the agency used...*
>
> *(National Adoption Day, 2005, p 13)*

A sensitively briefed professional photographer who could spend time with the child in their familiar setting would produce a much more real representation of the child. (Incidentally, if school photographs are used for looked after children, be careful to cover any identifying school badges – and make sure that whatever is on view in the background of a photograph is similarly anonymous.)

Video material must also be of a high quality

If poor footage gets in the way of people's connection to the child, the chances of a placement are diminished. Indoor film footage shot towards a window when it is impossible to make out the child's features; where there are distracting shots of the floor and the ceiling, and dizzying tracking shots as the child rushes around and the camera tries to keep up; where extraneous noise from the television and front door bell gets in the way of listening to the child or foster carer; or where fancy editing distracts the viewer – all of these detract from the central intention of the film.

Some of the worst shots are of petrified children stuck on a chair being asked what they had for breakfast or what they enjoy doing; or those where the child, self-conscious about the camera, shows off. These are so unnatural that they are excruciating to watch and entirely fail to convey what the child is really like. Far better to show the child eating breakfast and playing with their toys than to ask a small child for a description; and much better to involve the child in the filming so that in becoming familiar with the process, they lose their embarrassment.

Social workers seem to resist using professional photographers and film-makers. Apart from the costs, there is a view that "professional" might mean unnatural, glossy, stilted and child-unfriendly. Quite the reverse. A professional film-maker will know how to engage the child so that the final product is a natural portrayal of this individual young person. It may indeed all look so natural that the process is assumed to be easy to replicate. Far from it. If agencies do decide to make their own films, *Be My Parent's* guidelines for video-making (www.bemyparent.org.uk) will be helpful.

Films and (ideally) a variety of photographs can be used not only to attract a family in the linking process, but also at the next stage, when an identified family can sit with the social worker in the calmness of the office or the family's home and talk about the child in more detail. A good video adds immeasurably to the family's ability to imagine how it might be to live with this child.

But there is just one word of warning. Unfortunately some children will not only have viewed inappropriate film material, but photographs and videos may have been used abusively with them. Obviously, in such situations these media should be handled with even greater care, or avoided.

Always use film (video/DVD) when family-finding for a disabled child

The film may draw attention more explicitly than other media to the consequences of a child's impairment, which is of course necessary and has both positive and negative consequences. Some viewers will realise that they could indeed cope with this child; others will feel they cannot take on the extra issues which this particular impairment brings.

But the good news is that in a film, disability can be presented as a *part* of a child and not as the whole story. One short film shows a little girl playing happily in a variety of domestic settings. About halfway through the film, when she runs across the garden, it suddenly strikes the viewer that she has a slightly lop-sided gait. The voice-over (the foster carer) says that the child's cerebral palsy is so mild that it hardly affects her. This is the first the viewer knows about it. Had the child's disability been signalled at the start, or if it was mentioned in a profile without the film, it would have dominated the viewer's perception of her and diminished her appeal as an ordinary and lovely little girl.

Checklist for Tip 8

- **Make sure that you have very good, supportive and challenging supervision when you are responsible for finding a family for a child. This is emotional work.**
- **Think about the structure of the agency: does it contribute to or detract from the best possible family-finding service for children?**
- **You must know the child and his/her experiences and background history inside out.**
- **If you have taken over the case, ask for time to read all the files.**
- **Involve the child. If necessary, identify a colleague who can help you with this.**
- **Ask to go on a profile-writing course.**

- Pay particular attention to writing profiles of "disabled" children.
- Consider appointing one colleague per team as the profiling expert.
- Review the photographs you traditionally use and see if they can be improved and made more natural. Involve professionals.
- Use a variety of photographs where possible.
- Make a "promotional" video/DVD of each child. The material must be of a very high standard.
- Involve professional film makers and editors if possible – but definitely for children who are disabled or in other respects "hard to place".

TIP 9

Feature the child in a wide variety of ways

This chapter is about seeking a particular family for *this* specific child. This is the crux of the entire family-finding business.

There are many ways to promote a child, and arguably all possible avenues should be explored concurrently in order to avoid delay. Some publicity will feature child models; but where real children are being promoted, all the usual permissions must be obtained and precautions taken. At the point of writing this guide, there is some debate about the legality of featuring a child whose case is still in the court arena, and a current, though hopefully not indefinite, restriction in Scotland on using photographs. Staff will therefore need to check carefully what is legally possible in their country and what is the view of their local court.

Think outside the box!

There are a variety of avenues to be explored when family-finding for an individual child, which broadly fall into either of two perspectives: category matching and carer-led linking – plus, for the brave, child-led linking.

Category-matching

This is the traditional classification method where social workers make the link between a family's abilities/wishes, on the one hand, and the "kind of child" on the other (Cousins, 2003). This method is called "social worker-led" or "category-matching". This is based on the family, during the home study, identifying what "kind of child" they think they could take. It is essentially hypothetical, though social workers will have provided case scenarios during training for people to think about.

One of the least helpful methods is the "tick-box list" from the old Form F Part 1. This list identified 42 "specific matching considerations" or preferences, and asked the prospective carer to indicate "positively interested", "not interested" or "limited interest" in, for example:

- a child with specific medical needs;
- a child with mobility difficulties;
- a child who has been neglected;
- a child who may display overt behavioural difficulties;
- a child with foetal alcohol symptoms;
- a child who may have been physically abused;
- a child who is likely to have difficulty in bonding with carers over time.

This list, now redundant but occasionally still found to be in use, was open to misunderstanding and misinterpretation; made families feel uncertain and guilty; invited manipulation; and was such a blunt instrument that families often ruled themselves out for children whom they could in fact have parented. Most items on the list depend upon degree and nuance, and are ill-served by a simple tick in one box or another.

Category-matching also depends upon the child being classified by a shortlist of characteristics. These are usually determined by the common features on prospective families' wish lists, and for this reason, factors like learning difficulty, vision-impairment, contact with birth parents and so on, which families usually wish to avoid, are highlighted when a child is being classified. People rarely (if ever) state that above all they would like a child who laughs at silly jokes or adores hamsters: the focus is normally on aspects which are perceived as negatives, such as:

- has a slight speech delay;
- is unlikely to make relationships easily;
- has hepatitis C;
- has parents with a history of mental illness;
- may display sexualised behaviour;
- has mild cerebral palsy and epilepsy which is well-controlled.

For any particular child the statement may be true, and the writer has an obligation to be honest and describe the child realistically, but it is inevitable that such a statement will overshadow everything else which is said about him or her. The child has been reduced to a simplified label with no chance to show what they are really like in the round.

Carer-led linking
The other method turns this on its head: it is where families see photographs, short films and material about children (in, for example, *Be My Parent*, *Children Who Wait* and *BMP online*) and simply feel a response – positive or otherwise. The most radical extension of this is Activity Days, described below, where prospective carers actually meet the children.

A family who responds warmly to a child's details may or may not already be approved, but could be fast-tracked through the home study with that particular child in mind. Using this carer-led perspective, social workers lose their key role as broker in the link, but bring all their skills to bear in working with the family on whether this is indeed a good match. This is not, as some people fear, adults randomly choosing children based on a wave of emotion: the crucial ingredient is the careful assessment of the "fit" by the social worker in discussion with the family.

For clarification: a distinction can be made between the link and the match: in the carer-led approach, chemistry creates the link and robust assessment confirms the match.

Child-led

This is added to be provocative: social workers are probably not yet ready to allow young people to choose the prospective carers, rather than the other way round – but this would be a truly child-led approach. Families could produce their own profile (many do already) with photographs and drawings, and a selection of these profiles could be shown to a child who needs a family. Clearly, the child would be carefully prepared and supported by his or her social worker during the discussions, but a possible link may just emerge. There are many pitfalls, but nothing would be more compelling for future carers than to know that the child positively responded to them and wanted them to be his or her new family.

What now follows are the various different avenues which agencies should explore if children are to be given every chance of a permanent family.

1. Explore the child's network

Other than relatives and close friends, the child's wider network can be overlooked. Familiar people and places are better than unfamiliar ones, and the child will be known already just for who they are and not through a third-party description. This is especially important for disabled children. It has already been suggested that, if it is feasible, setting up a Child Appreciation Day to include members of the child's wider network may in itself lead to a link.

Contacts who might prove valuable in family-finding are, therefore:

- the child's existing care network: social workers, foster carers, short breaks carers, child-minders;
- education setting: teachers, teaching assistants, playground or dinner staff, school nurse and so on;
- health setting: nurses, doctors, paramedical staff;
- church network;
- families of the above who happen to have met the child (word-of-mouth is a powerful recruiter).

Any setting where there are public servants doing people-focused work might also prove useful places to feature the child.

2. Review the approved families in your agency and those currently being assessed

Each agency will have its own list of approved carers. As was stated earlier, adoptive families are no longer approved for a limited category (they are either approved or not approved) – which should release them to be proactive in identifying a child themselves. However, the agency will no doubt have developed a system of classification for their approved families (and children) in order to manage the linking process.

It is of course important to bear in mind the families who are currently coming through the preparation and home study process. It is just possible that one of them may be suitable for a child who is waiting. Regularly telephoning colleagues in neighbouring agencies with a freshly updated list of families and children is a time-consuming but allegedly effective way of making links. A more direct approach may be more efficient – if all agencies in a consortium could circulate photographs and details of children to all the approved and "in process" families within the consortium.

With interagency fees being a potential disincentive to looking out-of-agency for a family, it is inevitable that family-placement teams are tempted to wait for a family in-house. This causes delay. The heavy cost of keeping a child in foster care (particularly in the care of a private provider) never seems to be taken into consideration – presumably because different budgets are used for family-finding and temporary care. A more rational approach is needed.

3. Contact the Adoption Register

The Adoption Register works by using a combination of computer classification and Register staff who scrutinise the constant flow of families and children on their database. Between December 2004 and September 2007 the Adoption Register was instrumental in matching 433 children with adopters. All children for whom adoption is the plan should be referred by local authorities in England and Wales to the Register within three months, as long as the legal consents have been obtained and no local link is being pursued. Prospective adopters are referred three months after approval if a match locally has not been identified, or sooner if the agency and the family wish. The family must agree to the referral, and may from time to time check whether their details have been sent out for consideration; also they may ask Register staff for advice via the adopters' help line.

There are currently around 4,000 children waiting to be placed in families, of whom about 1,500 were on referral to the Register during 2006–2007. Twelve hundred families were on referral during the same period. It is very important that this invaluable tool should be used.

Any drawbacks are those intrinsic to a classification system, however sophisticated. An additional problem is the fact that the Register is set up only to create adoption links, not permanent fostering.

4. Use your consortium exchange system

Where agencies cannot come up with an in-house family for a particular child, it makes sense that a placement should be sought from a neighbouring authority. As discussed earlier, many authorities have come together into consortia, which are proving very effective in joint family-finding.

Unless there are serious child protection considerations, it is much better for a child not to be placed entirely out of area. For one thing, contact with relatives and friends will be easier to manage. Communication between authorities post-placement should, theoretically, also run more smoothly as workers are likely to know each other from regional meetings and training sessions.

5. Use informal networks

The serendipitous effectiveness of coffee breaks and lunch-times to provide the milieu in which placements are brokered cannot be ignored. Many a training workshop has seen child X being discussed for family Y when workers get chatting together over refreshments. These are golden opportunities!

6. Refer the child to family finding newspapers/magazines

The most effective publicity formats for child placement over many years have been the publications which feature photographs and profiles of children, such as *Be My Parent* (BMP) and *Children Who Wait*. These publications make distressing reading and are hugely powerful. *Be My Parent*, published across the UK 12 times a year, and often containing over 200 profiles of waiting children, was responsible, in 2005–06, for the placement of 236 children – an impressive tally. Black and minority ethnic children in particular have been placed very successfully this way. *BMP* is available to subscribers and agencies but is not, for obvious reasons, widely available among the general public. If a prospective adopter or carer is interested in a child, they contact *BMP* staff who will then put them in touch with the child's social worker. *Children Who Wait* operates slightly differently: agencies refer children (childrenwhowait@adoptionuk.org.uk) but prospective carers contact the agency directly if they are interested in a particular child.

This newspaper format fits perfectly the model described above as carer-led: the subscriber may just have a simple human response to a child and then ask for more details. If several people enquire about the same child, the child's agency must manage the next step sensitively so that the enquirers who are less suitable are not deterred from the entire process. If someone replies who seems possible, the child's social worker or family-finder must act quickly to find out more, contact the family's agency, and arrange a joint visit to discuss the child.

Respond quickly to expressions of interest
As with all publicity, there must be workers on hand to respond quickly to anyone who contacts them about a child.

> *Over half of the 442 respondents who told us about their experience of contacting social workers to enquire about featured children found it to be a negative experience...'You can't get hold of them';*
>
> *'They do not return calls'; and 'Their attitude is sometimes rude or upsetting.'*
>
> (Be My Parent, 2004)

This is corroborated by other research in Simmonds (2001) and Cousins (2006).

Fast track assessments if necessary

If the responding family is not already approved, but seems a possibility, a fast-track assessment should be arranged either by the child's agency or by commissioning a nearby agency (depending upon distance and staff resources). *Be My Parent* staff will explain the process in more detail and provide written guidance (www.bemyparent.org.uk).

7. Refer the child to *Be My Parent online*

It is now possible to extend the opportunities afforded by newspapers and magazines into the world of cyberspace. The internet version of *Be My Parent*, and similar ventures by individual agencies, can provide prospective carers with infinitely more information about waiting children, and many more chances, through multiple photographs and film clips, of enabling the essential chemistry to happen. The more space there is to allow the real child to shine through, the more chance for families to respond.

Concerns about the safety of highly sensitive information being available on the internet have perhaps deterred some agencies from embracing this medium and these concerns have had to be taken seriously (Barnett, 2005). But with the proper, rigorous safeguards in place, the internet gives children further chances to have a family. For children's sake, this opportunity cannot be missed.

8. Use the local press or specialist publications which reflect the child's interests

It is fairly rare for children to be featured in the national press – mainly because it is so expensive. Some national newspapers will offer space free of charge, and this is of course worth trying in the right circumstances. National minority-ethnic publications, the Faith press and specialist magazines which might attract people-minded people are worth exploring to see if they will feature specific children. If a child loves football or collecting stamps, think about a feature in the local club supporters' magazine, or stamp magazine. These ideas have really worked for some children.

Get some media training

The local press and media are always worth approaching because local stories, particularly about children, are their bread and butter. Social work staff must be prepared to speak on radio and television if necessary. For many, this is extremely daunting, but if this is a chance to talk about a child, you have to do it. You won't necessarily be star material the first time, but you will get better at it!

9. Provide profiles and features about specific children for National Adoption Week (NAW)

National Adoption Week is a really good opportunity to feature a specific child both in the local and possibly the national media. NAW staff are always keen to know of waiting children in the run-up to this autumn event. Although the week is a celebration of adoption and a chance to spread the word, individual stories of children are invaluable in giving the overall message a personal touch. Use this opportunity.

10. Go to "exchange days"

Several consortia of agencies have begun to run special exchange events where they feature some of their waiting children and invite all their approved adopters and carers to view the material. Each agency will have a stall, staffed with family placement and publicity workers, and there will be individualised material – photographs, posters and artwork – about each child they are promoting, often displayed attractively on large poster boards. The potential families will circulate around the room to view the children's material and talk to staff. Sometimes a small laptop film about a child is available to view on the stall. Often a time-slot is offered in order to even out the pressure on staff who will be available to talk in detail about any child whom the prospective carers feel they respond to.

The Adoption Register also runs these events across the country, with considerable success, particularly the specialised events aimed at placing black and minority ethnic children. In 2006, two events were run specifically for black, Asian and mixed heritage children and adopters. As a result, 22 children from the Register were placed with families. General events run in conjunction with local consortia have also led to children being placed for adoption and as many as 18 children (not from the Register) have been placed by agencies as a result of a single day's event.

Exchange days not only contribute to making placements for children, but also give prospective carers and adopters a taste of the reality of finding a suitable match.

11. Run "video profiling" events

In some ways, video profiling events are similar to exchange days, but there are crucial differences.

Video profiling events, which are founded on work developed in the 1970s and 1980s by staff at Parents for Children, have been adapted enthusiastically by agencies more recently. Northamptonshire call them "Parents for Children" evenings, and the four boroughs which make up Adoption in the Black Country use the term "Meet the Children" events. However, "video profiling" will be used here as it conveys that video footage is key to this method (though videos are of course rapidly being overtaken by DVDs).

How do they work?

Essentially, the meetings are usually in two parts: first there is an opportunity for prospective carers to view photographs, profiles and written material on the waiting children which are displayed on tables and poster-boards around the room. Then there is a cinema-style presentation to the whole audience about each child in succession: a two–three minute individual film clip showing the child engaged in a variety of activities. The families have in their hands a list of the children, and they can jot down their reactions as they see each short film. Probably no more than 25 films can usefully be shown in one evening – but around this number seems to be optimum if 50–70 people attend as they do, on average, in Northamptonshire.

Potential adopters and carers come to the meeting by invitation only. Agencies have developed different practices about whom to invite: some welcome carers who have completed the initial processes – attended an information evening, been visited at home at least once by a family placement worker, and expressed an interest in making a formal application. Other agencies only invite approved carers. The advantage of inviting people early in the approval process (though not too early) is that, should a possible link emerge, the family can be assessed quickly. As they go through the home study, much discussion will centre upon the needs of the child in question and the family's emerging views about parenting this child. Specific support needs can also be identified realistically. However, should it become clear that this is not the child for them, their approval, once finalised, would still stand: they are not tied to this child.

Some people question whether prospective carers feel more openly in competition with each other at these events than they would do if matches were being made without their knowledge. They may do. However, with sensitive support from staff most people are able to cope with a process which has to be focused on what is right for each child.

The results
The best results from these events seem to be where quite a large number and a good range of children are featured. When, after one such occasion, an agency was disappointed at the response, staff realised that they had featured mostly boys aged 5–10. At the next event they presented a much wider variety of children and the response was much better. Also, if the "audience" is predominantly from a particular minority ethnic group, children from these communities must be featured.

Most agencies that have recently embarked upon these events are keen to continue, and some claim not only considerable success in finding families for hard-to-place children, but also that the method is more cost-effective than other avenues.

- A bonus for Gateshead was the feedback from participants that showed that not only had 100 per cent enjoyed the event, but 40 per cent said they would now consider adopting an older child or sibling group because of the event (an additional 40 per cent were already considering such children).
- Staffordshire also emphasised this point: 'It brings home the reality of children to adopters and gets them to explore children outside their comfort zone. Therefore we may have people thinking about sibling groups or larger sibling groups when they were not before.' Following recent meetings, Staffordshire have placed, among other children, two boys aged eight and seven, an 11-year-old boy, a seven-year-old boy, and a 10-year-old girl. Interestingly, the event itself may be the catalyst for some children being offered a

permanent home with their current foster carers who suddenly realise that they are about to lose them: this was the case with a single boy, a sibling group of two and a sibling group of three.

- Adoption in the Black Country has run three meetings, and aim to hold an event twice a year. They have placed 10 children, a number of whom have some form of disability, and including three sibling groups.
- Through their Parents for Children video profiling events, which have been running since 2001, Northamptonshire have permanently placed over 70 per cent of the children featured (171 out of 235), with an average disruption rate of only three per cent. One of the many useful lessons they have learned over this period is that the phone number of the adoption team, and not the children's social workers, must be given as the contact number for families who wish to pursue interest in a particular child – and that the adoption staff must be the ones to continue co-ordinating the follow-up.

Research shows that the most successful adopters and permanent carers are flexible about the "kind of child" they want. There appears to be mounting evidence that video profiling events offer these open-minded people the maximum opportunity to respond to children. Prospective carers, quite unexpectedly, sometimes seem to "recognise" the right child. No one else can predict which features in a child suddenly spark a connection for the adults: for one couple it was that the little boy was wearing a scout uniform, which chimed with their own interest in youth work and scouting; for another family, a child simply looked like another family member and seemed immediately to belong. These are the incidental and serendipitous advantages of this method.

Some agencies are sufficiently large to run these events solo; some work alongside neighbouring agencies and share the task. The films, once made, can be used for a variety of purposes as well as this meeting: a shortened clip can be referred to *Be My Parent online*; the longer film can be used in more reflective circumstances at home with family members and the child's social worker; and the films are a priceless gift for the child's future life story memory box, providing a record of their time in foster care.

Specially made videos/DVDs can be commissioned through *SeeMe Films* (www.bemyparent.org.uk).

12. Take the plunge and run an "activity day"

Activity days are where families and children who are each "waiting" all meet each other.

> *It is possible...to organise an outing for a group of children who need families, and to prepare a group of families to join children in a day of activities. These activities may involve nothing more than playing in a soft environment, sharing meals, going for a walk and keeping tired children occupied.*
>
> (Argent and Kerrane, 1997, p 34)

Sometimes these events go by the name of "adoption picnics" or "adoption parties" but are more accurately "getting to know you" events. Some fell into disrepute in the US where they were described as "beauty contests". Nevertheless, if they are properly organised, they can clearly be an effective way of achieving a link. If prospective carers come with an open mind and then just respond to an individual young person whom they meet in the flesh, an unexpected placement may emerge. With this very direct method, the child becomes known to the prospective carer as a real person who happens to have a specific difficulty.

> *I'd always wanted to adopt...I never thought about disability till I saw the photos of disabled children who needed families...then I was invited to an activity day to meet some of the children. They said 'When Adam comes we'd like you to sit with him and give him lunch'...I wasn't too happy about it.*

> *Adam was the last one to arrive and they brought him over to me in his wheelchair and left him with me...Oh my goodness! So I picked him up and put him on my lap and he got hold of my hand and he moved it to the table and I gave him some food. He put it in his mouth and I looked at him and I said: 'Oh, he's lovely'. That was it really; I was just gone.*
>
> *(Argent, 1998, p 5)*

This is a vivid example of an adopter having an open mind about "what kind of child" and then just responding unexpectedly to an individual young person.

Checklist for Tip 9

- Think about using the carer-led perspective of family-finding.
- Use items 1–12 in this chapter as a checklist for each child.
- Respond quickly to expressions of interest wherever the child is featured.
- Fast track assessments if necessary.
- Keep in regular contact with colleagues in neighbouring agencies.
- Use the special interest magazines reflecting the child's favourite hobbies.
- Get some media training. The first time in front of the microphone or camera is the worst.
- Set up a video profiling event.
- Take the plunge and run an activity day.
- Believe that chemistry can work!

TIP 10

Make a good match

Earlier in this book, the distinction was made between identifying a link and making a match. This final chapter explores how judgements are reached about whether the principal players in the "link" are likely to be suited to each other for the long term: the match. Unfortunately, methodology in this area is relatively undeveloped.

Because this chapter brings together the two strands – prospective carers and child – there will be some interweaving of issues already touched upon.

Historically, because of the stigma of adoption, the intention of any match was to hide the fact of the non-blood tie. Matching methodology, such as it was, therefore emphasised physical resemblance as the foremost criterion. Things have moved on, but very little research has contributed to the endeavours of agencies to make strong, compatible placements. The lessons learned have largely come from studies about disruptions and "outcomes": we tend to know more about what goes wrong than what goes right (see Quinton *et al*, 1998; Dance and Rushton, 2005; Argent and Coleman, 2006).

Learn from disruptions

Disruptions are among the most highly charged events in family placement work, with everyone feeling angry with someone else. We know that some of the unalterable facts of children's lives, such as abuse, being split from brothers and sisters, preferential rejection and periods in care which lead to major behavioural problems all conspire to put a placement at risk, with the greatest risk factor being the age of the child. This much is known. We also know that placements made with undue speed and adopters who voice doubts which are ignored indicate a risky match.

Certain factors will help: openness, flexibility and reasonable expectations in the carers; placement support; good preparation of both child and family; interagency co-operation; and careful introductions. Adoption by foster carers is known to reduce the risk of disruption, but whether or not people already have parenting experience does not seem to be a factor in disrupted placements.

But when we set the child's risk factors against the prospective carers' (the match), we enter less familiar territory. Particular parenting styles may be suitable for certain children (evaluated through the Attachment Style Interview mentioned in Chapter 5). Household composition is a risk factor: Quinton warns against placement with established children (Quinton et al, 1998). Highly educated carers with unrealistic expectations should only be matched after careful account is taken of a child's abilities. In whichever respect prospective adopters' expectations are disappointed, and particularly where they feel obliged to "stretch" to accommodate the agency's wishes rather than their own, there is a potential recipe for difficulties.

On the whole, the lessons for the assessment, preparation and support of prospective carers are easier to see than pointers for matching. Probably the most useful advice is to be aware of what research continually reveals about all these complex dynamics.

Listen to children

As with so much else, hearing the child's view about how they would like to live and about an identified family should be part of everyday practice. It is usually unhelpful to ask what kind of family a child would like as their fantasy prescription can rarely be delivered. However, the following questions may generate a useful discussion which not only provides the social worker with insights but also prepares the child further for the coming changes.

- What do you want a new family to know about you?
- What things are really important to you?
- What scares you?
- What makes you laugh?
- When we find a family that we think is the best for you, is there anything you would like us to ask them?

Listening to children is time-consuming and often painful work. Tools are needed for this skilled task, the most precious of which are social workers themselves.

Begin with the assessed needs of the child

In assessing a potential match, the starting point is the needs of the child. Chapter 7 showed that the priority areas for consideration are likely to be:

- the route to permanence: adoption, permanent fostering or special guardianship;
- placement together with, or apart from, siblings;
- ethnic matching;
- broad decisions about contact;
- geographical location (sometimes).

Chapter 7 also advocated that care should be taken to avoid a rigid prescription of what would constitute the "right family". Such stipulations, often unsupported by objective evidence, will rule out matches which might be suitable, and may leave no families for the child at all. Personal preference and even prejudice can creep in: nothing else accounts for the fact that disabled approved carers are frequently ruled out at the matching stage. The issue of class is even more subterranean, and is not even talked about.

Confront received wisdom

It is therefore vital that social workers considering a match for a child keep an open mind about the kind of family who could be suitable.

- Believing that the child "must be the only child" or "must be the youngest" will rule out families with a structure which might work for this child; the "two-year rule" (the gap between children) is advisable, but there can be exceptions.
- Single carers with skills and supports are known to do well: it is foolish to rule them out.
- Some childless people have the skills to manage extraordinary challenges.
- Not only people with experience of disability can care for a disabled child.
- There is an unspoken view that disabled adults should be matched only with disabled children, regardless of objective assessment.
- Many BME children wait for a very long time for a new family because an exact ethnic match is proving elusive.

Remember: there is no such thing as a perfect match

Sometimes the key requirements of the child's plan may compete to such an extent that compromises have to be made. Occasionally, "race" and disability combined make a really good match impossible: it is known that BME disabled children are more likely than BME not-disabled children to be placed with a white family. Sometimes placement with siblings is the stumbling block; sometimes, as discussed earlier, adoption as a fixed plan can prevent an otherwise suitable permanent placement. In all these examples, where there are few choices, something has to give.

Staff must therefore accept that there is rarely such a thing as a perfect match. Some children may wait a very long time for a match which is actually unachievable, and some may never have a new family because of this. For children who in reality are unlikely to attract very much interest, why not welcome anyone who responds, and work from there?

Devise agency guidelines for matching

Where complex issues have to be juggled, having a set of guidelines is helpful. Some agencies have devised structures such as the edited version from Warwickshire Social Services (below), which provides a useful checklist for any discussion about matching. Each of the following issues would be explored in relation to the child.

- Background factors and issues which could have implications for future development.
- Child's current understanding and feelings about the past and about the permanence plan.
- Identity.
- Attachment.
- Abuse and neglect.
- Behaviour.
- Health and disability.
- Education.
- Contact.
- Needs of siblings.
- Other children in the new family.
- Post placement support.
- Financial issues.

In each instance, two questions would be asked:

- What are the child's needs arising from this issue?
- Does this family have the particular resources to cope in this respect?

Another example of a matching format from Bristol Social Services is found in Byrne (2000).

Set up a standing committee to consider matches

In some agencies, matches are considered only by the social worker and team manager before being presented to panel. This is a big responsibility, and a wider range of views should be canvassed. Setting up a small "matching" group or standing committee which can be convened quickly is helpful.

Assess the support needs

Foster carers will assume that an ongoing relationship with the local authority will ensure continued support. Special guardianship has no such guarantees, and future support will be at the agency's discretion. In adoption cases, prior to the match being presented to the panel, the support needs of the family and of the child must be assessed, and proposals about how the support will be provided must be confirmed in the Adoption Placement Report. There is also a requirement on the child's local authority, at the adopters' request, to assess support needs up to three years after an adoption order, but the actual provision of support is at the council's discretion. After three years, the responsibility passes to the local authority where the family is living. Financial support, however, remains with the child's authority and will continue for as long as the family qualifies for it.

Value the panel's role in matching

The panel has a crucial role in scrutinising proposed matches and support plans as they can often apply a wider view and a fresh range of skills. Local authority panels will already know the child and may have been the panel which approved the carers. In considering the match, they bring the two perspectives together. Education advisers on the panel are particularly valuable, especially if the child is to be placed in the local school system which is known to the panel member; but also in commenting to the family on aspects of the child's attainments. Similar advantages are to be gained from the medical adviser and from other specialists such as panel members from minority ethnic groups.

Although voluntary agencies have no statutory duty to recommend matches, those which choose to do so contribute "added value" to the process. Their knowledge of the family, inevitably superior to that of the local authority responsible for the child, is invaluable. While always mindful of the child's needs as paramount, the voluntary agency panel also acts as a second line of protection for the prospective family, through double-checking that all the information on the child is available and understood. Ultimately it is in children's best interests to have their future plans considered by as many wise people as possible.

Once a family has been identified – provide information

One factor is consistently clear from research: where a link has emerged, the family must be fully informed about the child before they make a commitment (and of course well before they meet the child). The necessity to give information cannot be stated strongly enough. Confidentiality issues need to be revisited and care taken not to disclose information about the parents which is not relevant to the child – it is not just the child's life which is being exposed. "Boundary disputes" can occur, however, where information seems to belong to more than one person. With this caveat, as full and frank an exploration as possible about the child's early experiences and current state is vital, involving advice from specialists where necessary. There will always be future surprises, but these need to be minimised at this stage.

Where disruptions occur, the most common complaint is that the family did not know enough about the child. Even where information is imparted, workers need to ensure that the child's history and experiences are not just heard but understood. One example from practice is a family which, a year after the placement, when things started to go wrong, seemed unaware of the very damaging experiences their adopted child had endured. These were facts which the professionals back at the office knew about in detail: a typical shocking "case". It seemed impossible that the adopters had not been told; one would have to wonder what exactly they had really heard and understood.

The notorious "Essex case" (Cullen, 2004) has heightened awareness about giving full information to prospective carers. In this particular case, the adopters claimed damages from the local authority for failing to tell them the extent of the child's difficulties. We have learned important things from this but nevertheless social workers need to temper enthusiastic openness with caution. Laudable though it is to explain possible problems in detail, this may lend undue weight to developmental difficulties or impairment. As children mature, not all outcomes will be problematic and a balanced approach is crucial.

However, sharing information so that prospective carers understand why children might behave as they do can to some extent ease the task of managing the problematic behaviour, and reduce the stress.

Checklist for Tip 10

- **Learn from disruptions – they tend to show the risk factors.**
- **Listen to children.**
- **Begin with the assessed needs of the child.**
- **Be open minded about what might constitute the "right**

family" for this child.
- Confront prejudice and received wisdom about prospective carers: they are all badly needed.
- Devise agency guidelines for matching.
- Set up a group or "standing committee" to consider matches.
- Assess and confirm the provision of support before a match is finalised.
- Value your panel's advice on matches.
- Voluntary agencies: bring matches to panel even though not legally required to do so.
- Give as much information as possible to the proposed family.

The stages beyond the match are not the subject of this book. Hedi Argent, in her *Ten Top Tips for Placing Children in Permanent Families* (2006) has comprehensively covered the vital aspects of introductions and moving in, supporting placements, maintaining continuity and promoting life-long openness, and her book is warmly commended to readers as a companion to this one.

Endpiece

This book is dedicated to Richard and Julie: young people for whom I tried to find permanent families many years ago, and failed. I think about them with enormous sadness. At the time I thought I was pulling out all the stops, but looking back I wonder if I, and the system of which I was part, could have looked for families more widely, with more imagination and more absolute determination.

To present-day social workers and managers, I would simply say: do the utmost you possibly can to find each child a family – and then go the extra mile.

References

Argent H (1996) *The Placement of Children with Disabilities*, Practice Note 34, London: BAAF

Argent H (1998) *Whatever Happened to Adam? Stories of disabled people who were adopted or fostered*, London: BAAF

Argent H (2006) *Ten Top Tips for Placing Children in Permanent Families*, London: BAAF

Argent H and Coleman J (2006) *Dealing with Disruption*, London: BAAF

Argent H and Kerrane A (1997) *Taking Extra Care: Respite, shared and permanent care for children with disabilities*, London: BAAF

BAAF, Department for Education and Skills, Welsh Assembly Government (2006) *Adoption Register Annual Report*, London: Department for Education and Skills

Barnett D (2005) *Profiling Children on the Internet*, London: BAAF

Beckett S and Oni P (2005) *Featuring Children in the Mainstream Media*, London: BAAF

Beesley P, Hutchinson B, Millar I and de Sousa S (2002) *Preparing to Adopt: A training pack for preparation groups*, London: BAAF

Be My Parent (2004) *Be My Parent Subscriber Survey 2004*, London: BAAF

Betts B (2007) *A Marginalised Resource? Recruiting, assessing and supporting single carers*, London: BAAF

Bond H (2004) *Fostering a Child: A guide for people interested in fostering*, London: BAAF

Bond H (2007) *Ten Top Tips for Managing Contact*, London: BAAF

Byrne S (2000) *Linking and Introductions: Helping children join adoptive families*, London: BAAF

Calam R, Cox A, Glasgow D, Jimmieson P and Groth Larsen S (2005) *In My Shoes: A computer assisted interview for communicating with children and vulnerable adults*, User Guide, York: Child & Family Training.
(Available via training course: contact liza.miller@btinternet.com)

Commission for Social Care Inspection (2006) *Adoption: Messages from inspections of adoption agencies*, London: Commission for Social Care Inspection

Cousins J (2003) 'Are we missing the match? Rethinking adopter assessment and child profiling', *Adoption & Fostering*, 27:4, pp 7–18

Cousins J (2006) *Every Child is Special: Placing disabled children for permanence*, London: BAAF

Cullen D (2004) 'Local authority liability to adopters: duty of care in respect of provision of information about children's backgrounds', *Adoption & Fostering*, 28:1, pp 78–80

Dance C and Rushton A (2005) 'Predictors of outcome for unrelated adoptive placements made during middle childhood', *Child & Family Social Work*, 10, pp 269–280

Department for Education and Skills (2006) *Practice Guidance on Preparing and Assessing Prospective Adopters*, London: DfES Publications

Department for Education and Skills (2007) *Care Matters: Transforming the lives of children and young people in care*, London: Department for Education and Skills

Department of Health (1991) *The Children Act 1989 Guidance and Regulations Vol. 3*, Family placements, London: The Stationery Office

Department of Health (2000) *Assessing Children in Need and their Families: Practice guidance*, London: The Stationery Office

Department of Health (2001) *National Adoption Standards for England*, London: The Stationery Office

Kolb DA (1984) *Experiential Learning*, Englewood Cliffs, NJ: Prentice Hall

Leslie A (2001) *'Report of the Part 8 Review of Brighton and Hove ACPC of the care and protection of JAS (aged 4) who died on 24th December 1999'*, Brighton: Brighton and Hove Area Committee

Lord J (2006) *Adopting a Child: A guide for people interested in adoption*, London: BAAF

Lord J and Borthwick S (2001) *Together or Apart: Assessing brothers and sisters for permanent placement*, London: BAAF

Luckock B and Lefevre H (2008) *Direct Work: Social work with children and young people in care*, London: BAAF

Macaskill C (1985) *Against the Odds: Adopting mentally handicapped children*, London: BAAF

Mallon G and Betts B (2005) *Recruiting, Assessing and Supporting Lesbian and Gay Carers and Adopters*, London: BAAF

McFadden EJ (2004) 'Preserving the sibling bond', Presentation to IFCO Conference November 2004, Prague

Morris J (1995) *Gone Missing? A research and policy review of disabled children living away from their families*, London: Who Cares? Trust

Morris J (1998) *Still Missing? Volumes 1 and 2*, London: Who Cares? Trust

National Adoption Day (2005) *Foster Care Adoption in the United States: An analysis of interest in adoption and a review of state recruitment strategies*, Washington DC: National Adoption Day Coalition

National Foster Care Association (1999) *UK National Standards for Foster Carers* and the *Code of Practice on the Recruitment, Assessment, Approval, Training, Management and Support of Foster Carers*, London: NFCA

NSPCC (2001) *Two-Way Street: Communicating with disabled children and young people (video and handbook)*, London: NSPCC, Joseph Rowntree Foundation and Triangle

Oakwater HW (2003) 'A wish list', in Argent H (ed) *Models of Adoption Support*, London: BAAF, pp 26–47

Owen M (1999) *Novices, Old Hands and Professionals: Adoption by single people*, London: BAAF

Quinton D (2004) *Supporting Parents: Messages from research* (Chapter 5: Studies of foster care), London: Jessica Kingsley

Quinton D, Rushton A, Dance C, Mayes D (1998) *Joining New Families: A study of adoption and fostering in middle childhood*, Chichester: John Wiley

Rule G (2006) *Recruiting Black and Minority Ethnic Adopters and Foster Carers*, London: BAAF

Rushton A, Dance C, Quinton D and Mayes D (2001) *Siblings in Late Permanent Placements*, London: BAAF

Ryan T and Walker R (2007) *Life Story Work*, London: BAAF

Selwyn J (2005) 'An evaluation of one local authority's post box service', presented to BAAF Research Group, 13th January 2005

Selwyn J, Frazer L and Fitzgerald A (2004) *Finding Adoptive Families for Black, Asian and Black Mixed-Parentage Children: Agency policy and practice*, London: National Children's Home

Selwyn J, Sturgess W, Quinton D and Baxter C (2006) *Costs and Outcomes of Non-Infant Adoptions*, London: BAAF

Shah S and Argent H (2006) *Life Story Work: What it is and what it means*, London: BAAF

Simmonds J (2001) *First Steps in Becoming an Adoptive Parent: An evaluation of NAW 1999*, London: BAAF

Social Care Institute for Excellence (2006) *Knowledge Review 12: Teaching, Learning and Assessing Communication Skills with Children and Young People in Social Work Education*, www.scie.org.uk/publications/knowledgereviews/kr12.asp

Thomas C and Beckford V (1999) *Adopted Children Speaking*, London: BAAF

Triseliotis J, Borland M and Hill M (2000) *Delivering Foster Care*, London: BAAF

Wates M (2002) 'How unexamined attitudes discriminate against disabled people as parents', *Adoption & Fostering*, 26:2, pp 49–56

Useful organisations

British Association for Adoption & Fostering (BAAF)
Saffron House
6–10 Kirby Street
London EC1N 8TS
Tel: 020 7421 2600
Fax: 020 7421 2601
www.baaf.org.uk

Be My Parent
Address as above
Tel: 020 7421 2666
Fax: 020 7421 2660
www.bemyparent.org.uk

BAAF England
South England
Address as above
Tel: 020 7421 2671

Central and Northern England
Unit 4, Pavilion Business Park
Royds Hall Road, Wortley
Leeds LS12 6AJ
Tel: 0113 289 1101

BAAF Scotland
40 Shandwick Place
Edinburgh EH2 4RT
Tel: 0131 220 4749

BAAF Cymru
7 Cleeve House
Lambourne Crescent
Cardiff CF14 5GP
Tel: 029 2076 1155

BAAF Northern Ireland
Botanic House
1–5 Botanic Avenue
Belfast BT7 1JG
Tel: 028 9031 5494

Adoption Register
Unit 4, Pavilion Business Park
Royds Hall Road, Wortley
Leeds LS12 6AJ
Tel: 0870 750 2173
www.adoptionregister.org.uk

Adoption UK
46 The Green, South Bar Street
Banbury OX16 9AB
Tel: 01295 752240
www.adoptionuk.org

Adoption Today magazine
Contact details as above

Fostering Network
87 Blackfriars Road
London SE1 8HA
Tel: 020 7620 6400
www.fostering.net

Fostering Network Scotland
Ingram House, 2nd Floor
Glasgow G1 1DA
Tel: 0141 204 1400

Fostering Network Wales
Suite 11, 2nd Floor
Bay Chambers, West Bute Street
Cardiff Bay CF10 5BB
Tel: 029 2044 0940